"Donna's book is a powerful tool for parents who wa
are so vulnerable when they're alone online. We need to
gers so we can protect them."

—Lee

"Donna has been an effective advocate on behalf of cₙₙₐᵣₑₙₛ ₒₙₗₙₑ ₐₑₐₐ,
leader in calling attention to the responsibilities of companies, the community, and parents. By continuing to speak out and partner with the rest of the Internet community
to address the needs of children, Donna is helping all of us build a medium we can be
proud of."

—**Steve Case**, chairman and CEO, America Online, Inc.

"As parents, we have a responsibility to monitor our children's use of the Internet.
Ms. Hughes has presented us with a resource to . . . ensure that our children's experience using the Internet is a safe one."

—**Senator John McCain**

"Donna Rice Hughes has been on the forefront of the battle to make the Internet
safe for our children. This book will be a valuable resource for parents as they struggle
to raise children in a digital age."

—**Senator Daniel Coats**

"Donna Rice Hughes challenges parents to take charge of their children's Internet
use and 'bridge the technogeneration gap.' Regardless of their Internet knowledge, parents will find this book to be a positive, important resource."

—**Ernie Allen,** president, National Center for Missing and Exploited Children

"In understandable language the author has written a book on the high and low
roads of the Internet. It is must reading for cyberspace parents."

—**James Exon,** former governor and U.S. Senator from Nebraska

"When children have access to the Internet they truly have the world at their fingertips. As parents we need to recognize the dangers in cyberspace and understand how
the Internet works if we are to protect our children."

—**Congressman Tom Davis**

"Finally, a 'user friendly' resource for parents desiring to protect their children in
cyberspace! Donna understands the importance of reaching moms and dads who may
or may not be computer savvy. *Kids Online* is a must read for every parent!"

—**Carmen Pate,** president, Concerned Women for America

"Donna Rice Hughes is to be commended. This book is must reading for any parent
with cybersavvy children."

—**Josette Shiner,** president and CEO, Empower America

"Essential reading for parents concerned about the safety of their children's online experiences. This is the information parents need to know."

—**Bruce Watson,** president, Enough Is Enough

"The most comprehensive, informative, and 'user-friendly' source available today. This book is a MUST for today's caring parents!"

—**Dee Jepsen,** president emeritus, Enough Is Enough

"This book is invaluable. We owe it to our kids to take the steps outlined in the book. Good stuff, especially if your child is better at computer hijinks than you are!"

—**Bruce A. Taylor,** president and chief counsel, National Law Center for Children and Families

"A must-read. Written in easy-to-understand language—even for 'non-techies' like me. *Kids Online* will help *you* control cyberspace, instead of it controlling you and your family, so what are you waiting for? Pick up this book!

—**Ramona Cramer Tucker,** editor, *Today's Christian Woman;* executive editor, *Virtue*

"Simple, direct, and incisive, this book provides parents with tools to make the Internet a safer environment for our children to operate and learn in."

—**Charlie Condon,** attorney general, South Carolina

"A *must* for any parent with a cybersavvy kid. We all need to work together to make sure the Internet is an exciting avenue of discovery for our children, not a source of exploitation."

—**Congressman Bob Franks,** co-chairman of the Congressional Missing and Exploited Children's Caucus

"This book provides an easy-to-understand overview of a complex subject. Above the shrill media hysteria, Donna offers a reassuring voice of calm to confused parents. Her common-sense suggestions allow families to 'take back the Net'."

—**Jean Armour Polly,** Net-mom® and author of *The Internet Kids and Family Yellow Pages*

"*Kids Online* is the answer to an S.O.S. that will keep America's kids from becoming 'Roadkill on the Information Highway.' It arms adults quickly and to the point. The best concise help from a powerhouse of knowledge. . . . A one-stop read."

—**Michael S. Bradshaw,** CEO, Log-On Data Corporation

"*Kids Online* is invaluable as parents and educators alike struggle with the important issue of our children's safety on the Internet."

—**Dr. Terry Hitchcock,** president, EdView, Inc.

"*Kids Online* serves up practical cybersavvy, giving parents an enormous leg up in the battle to keep kids safe in the often dangerous world of cyberspace."

—**Laurie Hall,** author of *An Affair of the Mind*

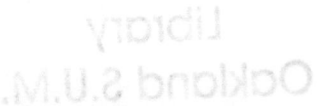

Kids Online

Protecting Your Children in Cyberspace

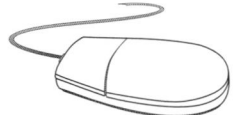

Donna Rice Hughes

with Pamela T. Campbell

Fleming H. Revell
A Division of Baker Book House
Grand Rapids, Michigan 49516

© 1998 by Donna Rice Hughes

Published by Fleming H. Revell
a division of Baker Book House Company
P.O. Box 6287, Grand Rapids, MI 49516-6287

Printed in the United States of America

Library of Congress Cataloging-in-Publication Data

Hughes, Donna Rice, 1958–
    Kids online : protecting your children in cyberspace / Donna Rice Hughes with Pamela T. Campbell
        p.   cm.
    Includes bibliographical references.
    ISBN 0-8007-5672-X
    1. Internet (Computer network) and children. 2. Parenting.
I. Campbell, Pamela T. II. Title.
HQ784.I58H84   1998
649'.1—dc21   98-7579

All names of persons whose stories are shared have been changed to protect their privacy.

For current information about all releases from Baker Book House, visit our web site:
http://www.bakerbooks.com

Contents

A Word
from the Author

I am often asked by the media and others why I got involved with the issue of pornography on the Internet. It's a long story, but here goes.

After years of living away from my spiritual roots, a journey that began with a series of little left turns, I found myself in 1987 in the middle of an international scandal, caught in the crossfire of press, politics, and public opinion. In despair I saw my life fall apart around me. Feeling helpless, hopeless, and at the end of my own resources, I realized that it had taken my falling on my rear end in front of the whole world for God to get my attention. He got it, and I recommitted myself to him and to my faith. Trusting the Lord, I prayed, "I know that in time you can heal the pain in my life and even use what appears to be a disaster for good."

Approximately seven years later I met Dee Jepsen. Dee was the president of Enough Is Enough (EIE), a nonprofit organization dedicated to addressing the sexual exploitation of children, women, and men by illegal pornography. We discussed the possibility of my joining the organization. At first, I thought, *This is not a good fit! The last things I want to get involved with are the media, politics, and sexually charged issues!* I was unsure. Could it be that God was leading me to become involved with the fight against illegal pornography?

When Dee shared with me that one of the harms of pornography is the rape myth—that when a woman says no, she really means yes—I realized for the first time that I might have been victimized by this at the age of twenty-two when I lost my virginity against my will. This incident was a catalyst that propelled me toward those left turns during my twenties. The realization that I too may have been negatively affected by pornography was the green light for me to take a step of faith and join Enough Is Enough.

At Enough Is Enough, I soon became aware of the pervasive problem of pornography in our society. Within weeks, a friend showed me the kind of pornographic content that is available in cyberspace. Through the Internet, adults and children can freely access illegal pornography that isn't even available to adults in XXX bookstores. Just as troubling, sexual predators can silently enter a family's home and interact with a vulnerable child via the Internet. Not only are children and families harmed by the growing pervasiveness of such online risks, but such misuse and pollution negatively impact the Internet itself. I became determined to help prevent such a valuable tool from being compromised by pornography and pedophile activity, which would in essence render the medium unusable to children.

It was essential to wake up the country to the dangers. I was convinced that if we could expose the harsh reality of online risks to children, we might be able to protect children from such dangers and at the same time fulfill a goal of EIE—change the way America thinks about pornography. I finally understood why God called me to this work, to be a part of his plan to bring public awareness and solutions to this massive problem confronting our culture. Protecting children in cyberspace is a responsibility that must be shared by the public, the technology industry, and law enforcement. The appropriate implementation of this strategy will protect children without infringing on rights established by the First Amendment.

After a year of plugging away, we helped to launch the issues of computer porn and pedophile activity into the headlines, and surprisingly I found myself working with the media and politics—the very same communities of people who had caused me so much pain in the past. As a result of this involvement, I've had an opportunity to be on the front lines of an issue that impacts all of us.

In the Old Testament the prophet Jeremiah writes to the exiles from Israel, assuring them that God has not forgotten them. He says, in fact, that despite their waywardness, God had for them a hope and a future (Jer. 29:11). I found this to be true in my life. God provided me a productive way to use my years of suffering. My commitment to the Lord combined with my understanding of the media, my entrepreneurial experience, and my awareness of the devastation of sexual exploitation have led me to champion children and fight to protect them from the dangers of pornography and predators in cyberspace.

It is my sincere hope that this book will serve as an awareness tool, a training manual, and a resource to empower all child advocates—parents, educators, librarians, industry leaders, law enforcement officials, politicians, community caregivers—to join together to make the Internet safe, educational, and entertaining. Our children deserve a protected space of innocence and nothing less!

For the sake of the children,
Donna Rice Hughes

Acknowledgments

This book is a compilation of what I've learned during my four-year tenure at Enough Is Enough. I am grateful for the many opportunities I've had while on staff at this worthwhile organization, under the leadership and support of my friend and mentor Dee Jepsen and the Board of EIE, to explore the uncharted waters of making the Internet safe for children.

I want to thank the following people who have had important roles in the journey that has brought me to write this book:

> My parents, my sister, Kathy, and my loving husband, Jack, for their willingness to trust God and me, to step forward into the public limelight on such a controversial issue and risk being scrutinized by the media all over again. Thank you for your support as I took the step of joining the staff of Enough Is Enough and for your backing when I went public with the message of the serious dangers posed to children online and the importance of making the Internet safe for children. If it had not been for your faith, encouragement, and sup-

port, I may have never had the courage to take these steps.

My faithful and supportive husband, Jack, for being my "plumb line" and sharing me with the work that has taken me out of our home so much of the time for the past four years.

My stepson, Sean, and my stepdaughter, Mindy, for helping me understand how *real* teenagers view these issues. Thanks, Sean, for not complaining about my "hogging" our home computer for two months to get this book written!

All my close friends, for their continued encouragement and support of me during the bad times and the good. And especially Mary Dorcmus who always instilled in me a sense of hope when my future seemed hopeless.

Nina May, for boldly believing in me and recommending that Dee Jepsen consider me for a position at EIE.

The staff at Enough Is Enough, for their commitment and dedication to addressing the sexual exploitation of children, women, and men by illegal pornography.

Nicky Ring, my faithful assistant and friend who has been my right hand for the past year and a half.

Cathy Cleaver and Bruce Taylor, for locking arms with me in our joint worthwhile effort to help put this issue on the map.

Jean Armour Polly, for her insightful edits on the manuscript.

Bruce Taylor, for his advice and legal edits on the manuscript.

Laurie Hall and Gene McConnell, for their help with chapter 4 and their willingness to use the pain pornography brought into their respective lives to teach us all that pornography is not a victimless crime.

Lorrie Faith Cranor and her assistant, Danielle Gall, for their edits on chapter 6.

Bruce Watson, for his edits on chapters 6 and 7.

Pam Campbell, for her patient, calm spirit throughout this most grueling process of birthing a book in two months.

Linda Holland, for her vision for this book and her unwavering pursuit of me to author it.

Mary Suggs, for her editing expertise and her commitment to excellence.

Robert Wolgemuth, for his guidance on my first book.

All those who served with me on the Internet Online Summit steering committee and checked their differences at the door for the sake of the children.

I would like to acknowledge the following for granting me permission to adapt and/or reprint their materials:

Child Safety Online, an overview of the issues concerning child safety online, prepared by a subcommittee of the Child Advocacy Working Group, 1997 Internet Online Summit: Focus on Children. December 1–3, 1997.

Victor B. Cline, *Pornography's Effects on Adults and Children,* published by Morality in Media, 475 Riverside Drive, #239, New York, NY 10115, 212-870-3222, fax: 212-870-2765.

Lorrie Faith Cranor (AT&T Labs—Research, Florham Park, NJ, lorrie@research.att.com) and Paul Resnick (The University of Michigan School of Information, presnick@umich.edu) *Internet Online Summit Technology Inventory* (November 24, 1997).

Get Cybersavvy, published by The Direct Marketing Association (DMA), 1120 Avenue of the Americas, New York, NY 10036-6700, 212-768-7277, http://www.the-dma.org.

Education Task Force Report for the 1997 Internet Online Summit: Focus on Children.

Wendy Lazarus and Laurie Lipper, *The Parents' Guide to the Information Superhighway*, published by The Children's Partnership, 1998, (with the National PTA and National Urban League).

Kathryn C. Montgomery, *Creating an Electronic Legacy for Our Children*, published by the Center for Media Education, 1511 K Street, NW, Suite 518, Washington, DC 20005, 202-628-2620, Fax: 202 628-2554, e-mail: cme@cme.org, http://www.cme .org/cme.

Parents Guide to the Internet published by the U.S. Department of Education, (November 1997), Office of Educational Research and Improvement, Media and Information Services, 555 New Jersey Avenue NW, Washington, DC 20208-5570, 800-USA-Learn, http://www.ed.gov/.

Take Action Manual, Library Action Manual, and *Internet Safety Kit*, published by Enough Is Enough, National Headquarters, P.O. Box 888, Fairfax, VA 22030-0888, 703-278-8343, Fax: 703-278-8510, http://www.enough.org.

Introduction

What do you know about the Internet? Is it a vague puzzle you'd rather not be involved in, a marvel of technology that you've heard can bring a world of knowledge right into your home, or a tool you're already using for research, entertainment, and communication?

Whether you're a computer whiz or a computerphobe, you may not be aware of the potential for both benefit and risk available on the Internet.

Here is the story of the negative impact that an unsupervised child's Internet access had on one family. Tracey tells the story.

In December 1996 my fourteen-year-old sister vanished without a trace, without a word to anyone in her family or circle of friends. Because she was such an "ideal" kid—honors student, intelligent, naive, and shy— we were terrified that she had been abducted by someone with malicious intent. She had never run away and she was an inexperienced girl who had never even been on a formal date with a boy.

We later learned that she had met in person with an adult man from the air force—one whom she had met only online in an Internet chat room. We learned this important information through the torn printouts of e-mail letters we found in her bedroom wastebasket.

The man identified in the torn e-mail letters had taken a leave from his air force base the same day my sister disappeared. He did not return to duty as scheduled. After an exasperating experience with certain branches of law enforcement, who insisted that fourteen year olds can take care of themselves, I had no choice but to contact the media in order to secure the safe return of my sister. Fortunately the media was interested in the Internet connection of my story.

In the following months, my entire family banded together to split up "talk show duty." We all knew that as the days passed, this man could be causing my sister to change irreversibly or, we feared, he could be harming her. On April 16, 1997, *The Maury Povich Show* aired a second piece on Internet-related disappearances. Their first show had brought one young girl home, but nothing in it led us to my sister. Though we were still hoping, many of us feared that she was no longer alive.

As a result of the second show, however, two coworkers of the man who had my sister called the producers of *The Maury Povich Show* and Child Quest International, a group that had stuck with us every step of the way. (Child Quest is a nonprofit organization devoted to the protection and recovery of missing, abused, and exploited children and at-risk adults. The organization was involved with this particular Maury Povich show.) Within hours, my sister was located and taken into military custody by the Air Force Office of Special Investigations, a branch of law enforcement that had shown compassion to my family during my sister's absence.

The ending to my story is joyful because my sister is home and resuming her young life as best she can. But there are a lot of issues we are still dealing with as a family—issues that will take a long time to understand and resolve.

Proactive Internet safety education and better supervision of Internet activity might have prevented this crime from occurring in the first place. My sister was not using a computer in her own home—it was in a room at my uncle's house next door. My family simply did not know that this sort of thing could happen over the Internet. We were unprepared, and my sister was easy prey. (Information taken from Tracey's Web site: http://www.webwisekids.com.)

Tracey's story is unusual only in that her sister was able to safely rejoin her family. Other families have not been so fortunate. Many have suffered tragic losses from similar Internet encounters. And while Tracey's story is a more extreme scenario than some, her concerns about Internet safety are well warranted.

In 1994, when I first went to work for Enough Is Enough (EIE), a nonprofit organization dedicated to addressing the sexual exploitation of children, women, and men by illegal pornography, EIE's primary targets were video, broadcast, print, and sexually oriented businesses. After a few weeks a colleague showed me the written descriptions of some of the pornography that is available via the Internet. I couldn't believe that such material, degrading beyond my comprehension, was circulating in the public spaces of this emerging medium. I was convinced that if we could expose the truth of the depths of depravity existing in the dark side of cyberspace, the public—regardless of their religious beliefs or political orientations—would be alarmed as well. I discussed my concerns with EIE's president, Dee Jepsen, and said, "The worst of the worst types of pornography are being delivered freely to anyone who has access to the Internet, including children. What even adults cannot get in pornography shops in New York or San Francisco, children can get for free on the Internet!"

From that point forward, as the communications and marketing director for EIE, I joined forces with other child advocates in pioneering national efforts to make the Internet safe for children. We are answering the challenges concerning the risks to children in cyberspace and working toward the implementation of solutions.

As a parent and an advocate for children, two major concerns about the Internet emerge for me. My first concern is that when children go online, they have easy access to every type of pornography conceivable. Once they've seen it, it can never be erased from their minds. My second concern is that the Internet makes it possible for pedophiles and sexual predators to have easy access to children, as in the case of Tracey's sister.

Just as our children need our guidance in other areas of their lives, they need our involvement, experience, and judgment when they go online. Let us heed the warning implicit in Tracey's story. Let it never be said that "we did not know that this sort of thing could happen over the Internet."

1

Bridging
the Technogeneration Gap

"Mom, can we get a PC?"

"What?" asked Susan, stirring from her study of the college catalog in her lap.

"Can we get a PC?" pleaded Lily. "You know, a personal computer for here at home."

"Well, I don't know. What would you do with it? Can't you work on one of the computers at school?"

"I could, but I can only get in the computer lab at the same time that Mrs. Arnold wants me in her art class. If we had a computer at home, I could do my homework and reports *here*. And Dad wouldn't have to work late every night. He could do some of his work at home. You could do stuff on it too! And if we get online, I can talk to my friends instantly, play games, send messages, and you can do your banking and grocery shopping on

19

it. You can even research where you want to go back to
school!"

"Whoa! Who needs a computer to do grocery shopping? And besides, a computer is expensive!"

"But it would be worth it! I know I could bring up my
grades if we had a computer. Plus, if you're going back
to school, you're not going to have as much time to go
to the bank and the grocery store. Think how much time
we'll both save!"

"I'll think about it, Lily."

Susan turned back to the college catalog, but the
words blurred in front of her eyes as she thought about
the possibility of doing her own college homework and
reports on a computer. *Maybe Tom **could** spend more
time at home if we had our own computer. It would sure
make things simpler, particularly if I could tap into the
university library. Lily is right. I could save a lot of time
by banking online, and I would like for her to have time
for more creative activities. But with all the news about
pornography, abductions, and stalking on the Internet, I
wonder how safe Lily—and I—will be if we go online.
How am I going to protect a ten year old who already
knows so much more than I do about computers and online services?*

Have you ever felt like Susan—comfortable with the
styles and tools of communication that you use with
friends, extended family, employer, employees, businesses, and community, and a little startled by how
quickly the worlds of technology and telecommunications are beginning to invade your comfort zone?

You are not alone!

For many of us, computers and telecommunications
are exciting but mystifying. Our children typically know
far more than we do about this new technology. While
we're still trying to figure out how to set that annoying

clock on our VCR, our children are clicking their way to exciting new worlds that didn't even exist when we were their age. Their fluent second language, which includes such words and phrases as *search engine, Web, USENET newsgroups,* and *e-mail,* sometimes adds to the generation gap between us. In addition, many of our computer-literate children have been exposed already to the benefits—and the dangers—of the Internet. How do we begin to bridge this gap so that we will be able to help our kids get ready for the Digital Communication Age of the next century?

In a message to parents, President Bill Clinton said it is critical that our children have our guidance as they learn to use the Internet. He went on to say:

> Although children can use the Internet to tap into the Library of Congress or download pictures from the surface of Mars, not all of the material on the Internet is appropriate for children. As a parent, you can guide and teach your child in a way that no one else can. You can make sure that your child's experience on the Internet is safe, educational, and enjoyable.[1]

As these new media change the way we communicate, advanced competencies will be required for the next generation of adults—our children—to compete in the workforce. If we do not encourage our children to become computer literate and to develop Internet savvy, we may be imposing on them an inability to be competitive in the future, highly selective job market. They may be "information poor" and at risk for poverty.

The challenge for involvement in these new global media may seem more difficult than any other we've faced before as parents, but many of the tools for responding to this challenge can be found in the chapters of this book. Let's face the challenge together.

The New Digital Age

Remember *The Jetsons* cartoon? George used to phone his wife and his face would appear on a large screen when she answered. I used to think this was an imaginative concept reserved for a space-age distant future.

While we're not yet able to live in satellite homes among the stars and fly little spacecars to work, we *are* able to communicate face-to-face around the world with the help of new global technologies. Just as my generation was influenced by the futuristic innovations of *Mission Impossible* and *Star Wars*, our children and their friends will be shaped by the converging technologies of the Digital Age. The rapid growth of technology, the proliferation of cable and satellite television channels, and the innovative developments in TV, telephones, and other communication technologies are combining to create dazzling graphics and an engaging interactive media environment that is easily accessed by our children. Web TV, cable, and direct broadcast satellite services, for example, bring the Internet into the living room and classroom via the television. AT&T's PocketNet mobile phone service offers wireless access to the Internet with both voice and data access. As the technologies of TV, computer, and telephone merge, our children may increasingly be able to reside in their own separate electronic worlds.

We deceive ourselves if we think these new global interactive media will not affect our homes, neighborhoods, places of business, schools, and culture—both positively and negatively. According to Dataquest Inc., a California market research firm, the number of personal computers hooked up to the Internet jumped 71 percent during 1997 to 82 million people and is expected to more than triple to 268 million by the year

2001.[2] More than four million children are already on-line in school.[3] Some researchers expect that number to grow nearly four times by the year 2000.[4]

In addition, many parents are beginning to understand how important computer skills are to educational success. I realized the importance of computer knowledge when I read that more than half of the new jobs in today's market require technological literacy. At the same time, not all parents can afford to buy a personal computer for their children. That's why the Federal Communications Commission (FCC) approved a rule (known as the E-rate) in May 1997 giving schools discounts in access charges to the Internet and telecommunications services. Public and private initiatives at the state and federal levels will help bring schools and libraries into the Digital Age and begin to provide electronic equity for all children.

The opportunity to work on a computer and go on-line gives children from all socioeconomic backgrounds the ability to find and use information, solve problems, and communicate with others, enabling them to improve their technological and informational skills. As the FCC follows through on its commitment to create more opportunities for low-income households, more people than ever before will have access to basic communications services that may have been previously unaffordable.

Whether you own a personal computer or not, whether your child is an experienced computer user or just getting started, he or she needs your involvement, experience, and judgment. My goal in this book is to help you learn what you need to begin closing the technogeneration gap, so that you can guide your child's use of the Internet and do all you can to protect him or her from the dangers inherent in it.

The Vocabulary of Computers

Computer literacy begins with understanding that the vocabulary of computers is derived from sources familiar to us.[5] For example, some computer language is borrowed from:

- transportation—*cruising, engine, navigating, super-highway, surfing*
- dining—*cookie, menu, server*
- common items from the environment—*links, mouse, Net, site, Web, Windows*
- library—*bookmarks, browser, home page*

Other computer language is descriptive of the movement or sounds made to do something on the computer: to click or drag the mouse, for example. Other words remind us of medieval manuscripts: *icon, scroll, cursor.* Throughout this book, you will find key computer terms in italics. If you're unfamiliar with these words and phrases, you will discover complete definitions and explanations in the glossary at the end of this book.

The Internet

When I refer to "getting online," I mean being connected to the *Internet.* Whatever you choose to call it—*cyberspace,* the *Information Superhighway,* the *Net*—the Internet is a giant network of computers that connects people and information around the world. It has a lot in common with other forms of communication:

- Like the U.S. Postal Service, the Internet allows anyone who knows your Internet address to send you a message. It's called electronic mail (or *e-mail* for short).

- Like the telephone, the Internet allows you to talk or chat with other people through *instant messages (IMs)* or by participating in online discussion groups.
- Like the library, the Internet contains information on a multitude of topics in a variety of formats, including books, magazine articles, videos, and audio and music recordings.
- Like the newspaper, the Internet gives you new information every day, including world, business, and financial news; stock reports; sports scores; travel information; entertainment; and ads.

In addition to words, one part of the Internet—the *World Wide Web* (*WWW* or *Web* for short)—is especially interesting because it includes pictures and sounds.

In this book I use the term *Internet* as a shorthand term for all the online services and networks, such as the World Wide Web—which is considered part of the Internet—and USENET and bulletin board services (BBS)—which are not technically part of the Internet but are accessed through an Internet Service Provider.

An Internet History Lesson

The Internet began in the 1960s as a U.S. Department of Defense communication network. Soon university researchers and professors began to use it to communicate with others in their field. Internet use really took off in the early 1990s with the arrival of graphic browsers to the Web, making it easier to find and view information online. Today millions of people throughout the world are connected to the Internet. No one—no country, organization, or company—is in charge of the Internet. It's growing and being changed by its users every day.[6]

Some Benefits of Getting Online

Educational Opportunities

A computer connected to the Internet brings a world of unlimited information and communication to your child's fingertips. By visiting educational sites on the Internet, your child can learn anything from history to math from online tutors who volunteer their time to help with school projects. No longer does your child have to go to an outdated encyclopedia to research a subject. On the Internet, he or she can access current information. For example, at the NASA site (http://www.nasa.gov/), your child can learn about the latest discoveries about the surface of Mars.

My education came from textbooks that were written years before I actually read them. Today the Internet can provide children with up-to-the-minute news, copies of important historical documents and photos, information on topics ranging from weather conditions to population statistics, and access to online museums and hands-on projects.

The Internet also is an extraordinary resource for parents and teachers. Information available on the Internet can come alive in the hands of a teacher as students research, for example, the origins of nations and planets, the history of the automobile, or the future of telecommunications. The Web maximizes research time and enhances the learning experience and knowledge retention through its interactivity, design, and content.

The Internet can benefit learning in another way—it can help you stay in touch with your child's school and teachers. By linking up to individual Web sites or communicating with schools and teachers through the use of e-mail, you can increase your knowledge of and involvement in what your child is learning. Spending time online with your child can help you expose your child to information and experiences that *you* value.

Reading Skills

Access to the Internet can improve your child's reading skills by providing interesting materials to read and suggesting additional reading. Some software programs can monitor every keystroke on the computer, track how a child thinks and feels, and create highly personalized program content designed specifically for that child. If used beneficially, such sophisticated tools could significantly improve a child's life. Research on computer-based learning has already demonstrated many of the benefits of these technologies.

Communication

As children use the Internet to connect with places around the world and exchange mail with electronic pen pals, they can learn about other cultures and traditions. No longer do they have to wait weeks or months for their pen pals' response—they can talk to their online friends and relatives every day in *real time* and for very little cost.

Live video conferencing is one of the most advanced technologies for communication. Real-time communication via video conferencing allows students to listen to and talk with experts from around the world.

Research

I've already mentioned some of the benefits of research in education. Your children can use the Internet to access libraries around the corner or around the world.

The Internet also provides passage to specific collections of information, online encyclopedias, the Library of Congress, reference materials, and experts in many fields.

Suppose your child is trying to decide which university to attend. Writing and requesting catalogs from each college can be costly and time-consuming. With access to the Internet, you and your child can find schools that meet your student's requirements and you can request admissions and financial aid information via e-mail in just a few hours.

Entertainment

Artwork, books, software programs, and games are all available on the Internet for you and your child to enjoy. Children can even participate in innovative and interactive games with players from the other side of the globe. However, just as you would at the local playground, you should supervise your child's play online.

Networking

The Internet offers thousands of *newsgroups*, each devoted to a special area of discussion. For example, fans of a certain type of music or literature and students interested in a particular field of psychology often have their own newsgroups. People send or *post* messages and responses on various topics to be read at any time, much like a bulletin board. E-mail and *chat rooms* are also Internet features that contribute to networking.

Some Risks of Getting Online

Similar to the print and film industries, the technology of the Internet is neutral in and of itself. But just as there are those in our community who have historically exploited others in print materials and films for their own profit, you and your child may discover some unsafe individuals, harmful content, and illegal activities in the Internet community. We will always have clever opportunists who abuse new media. In fact they are often the first to learn how to use leading-edge technology for the distribution of pornography.

Distribution of Pornography

With unrestricted access, any child with a computer and a *modem* can access pornographic material in seconds, and once it's been seen, the pornography can never be entirely erased from the mind. There is considerable evidence that children are being exposed to violent and sexually explicit content while online. We'll look at the nature and location of such material in chapter 3.

USENET newsgroups are notorious for harboring illegal pornography. In fact the oldest forum on the Internet for promoting the sexual exploitation of women is the newsgroup alt.sex.services (renamed alt.sex.prostitution). Postings from this newsgroup are archived into a Web site called "The World Sex Guide," which provides sex-related information and advice on how to find and buy prostitutes and children in over eighty countries.

One click on any newsgroup could take your child into a listing of free files that contain sexually explicit pictures, stories, and messages. And while video conferencing has its benefits for education and technology, it also provides a way to sell live strip shows over the Internet. No matter how hard we try, we cannot protect ourselves and our loved ones in a culture that permits deviant forms of illegal pornography to flourish.

In addition, many commercial pornographers operating sites on the World Wide Web post free teaser images on their sites, enticing Web surfers to subscribe to their services. By browsing the Web sites of these pornographers, children can view an enormous number of sexually explicit pictures without charge. Pornographers post and transmit free images knowing that children have access to them. And yet Web pornographers are some of the most innovative Internet leaders in developing privacy services and secure payment schemes. They certainly have the means, even through simple credit card or adult verification requests, to prevent children from viewing their pornography. The Children's Online Protection Act (1998) currently before the U.S. Congress would end this practice of free "teaser" images being made available to children by commercial pornographers operating on the World Wide Web.

Sexual Predators

Some people online believe that the laws regarding pornography can't or shouldn't apply in cyberspace; others feel that the anonymity of the Internet relieves them of responsibility for their actions. Just as disturbing as the pornography itself is the difficulty in protecting children from those people who derive sexual pleasure from anonymously viewing illegal pornography and who search for victims through conversations with unsuspecting kids on the Internet. Since chat rooms have become the playgrounds of the '90s, sexual predators lurk in those areas on the Internet in the hope of luring unsuspecting children into illicit sexual encounters.[7]

Misinformation and Hidden Messages

The Internet is an inexpensive, easy method of publishing information. Every Internet user is a potential publisher or "expert." Your child may have difficulty distinguishing truth from fiction in cyberspace. Children (and many adults) tend to believe everything they read and so are easily swayed by articles advocating pyramid schemes, racism, gambling, hate groups, and any number of other topics. While new technology and software have made strides in blocking out pornography, misinformation found in other places on the Internet is more difficult to block.

Internet sites such as www.schoolsucks.com and www.cheathouse.com, also known as "Evil House of Cheat," offer students an escape hatch from having to write term papers. They list thousands of papers on hundreds of topics ready to be downloaded twenty-four hours a day.[8] Many children have accessed information on how to make drugs or build bombs.[9]

Loss of Privacy

Another risk of the Internet is the possibility of you or your child losing your anonymity online through *cookies*, information you supply voluntarily when you register or fill out a form at a Web site. According to a recent survey conducted by the Center for Media Education, a children's media watchdog group located in Washington, D.C., roughly 90 percent of the major children's Web sites they surveyed solicit personal information about children.[10] Some sites use this information for their own purposes, but others sell the data to third parties and advertisers. For example, a child may apply for a free hamburger coupon online and thereby supply personal information that is sold to other sources. In one case, a journalist, using the name of a convicted pedophile and murderer, ordered and received a list of children's names from a marketing service. As a result, the Children's Privacy Protection and Parental Empowerment Act of 1996 was introduced into Congress by Congressman Bob Franks. This bill prohibits the sale of personal information about children without their parents' consent and it requires marketing services and other groups to have parental permission before using a child's name in any type of marketing information. At the time of this book's publication, this bill has not been passed by Congress.

Unscrupulous Vendors

With more and more kids online, more and more advertisers are marketing to them and seeking private information to better define their marketing strategies. While screening software and other technological tools may provide some solutions to this invasion of privacy, parents should not have to bear all the burden of protecting their children from manipulative and deceptive online business practices. In many of the online children's content areas, the lines between advertising, entertainment, and information are quickly disappearing. These electronic playgrounds invite children to come and play for extended hours with product "spokescharacters." Child development experts find such practices very troubling, since many children cannot distinguish fantasy from reality, do not recognize when they are being marketed to, and put a great deal of trust in these friendly, electronic authority figures.[11]

The Web also promises a whole new generation of interactive advertising that targets young people, particularly by beer, liquor, and tobacco companies. "It is not too difficult to imagine a fully animated Joe Camel sharing cyberspace with the likes of Chester Cheetah and Tony the Tiger."[12]

Development of Childhood Behavior Disorders

Major sociological changes in the nature of play, family, and parenting style have altered the experience of childhood for kids today. Computer usage has had a part in those changes. Children have the capacity to spend hours alone on the computer, exercising their imagination and developing problem-solving skills and creative thought. At the same time, excessive (as opposed to moderate) activity on the computer trains the brain to be unfocused and agitated. Research indicates that while traditional play trains the brain to be calm, focused, and relaxed, the activity in modern, high-tech play can cause the opposite effects, resulting in symptoms that resemble attention deficit hyperactivity disorder and oppositional defiant disorder. In addition, the impact of viewing violent images on the Internet may desensitize children to tragedies they encounter in real life while increasing aggressive behavior.[13]

While no authoritative studies have been completed to date, smaller studies indicate that some young teens may be suffering from internet addiction disorder (IAD). Psychologists debate whether IAD is truly an addiction, but some suggest that anyone who compulsively checks e-mail, obsesses about the next online session, and spends too much time or money online may be suffering from an out-of-control behavior.[14]

Conclusion

Are you disturbed by the risks of being online? I know I am! But I also know the benefits outweigh the risks, especially as parents exercise the necessary safety measures to protect their children online.

You'll probably find that many of the parents' guides on the market focus primarily on the positive aspects of the Internet while only briefly touching on some of the risks and the technological solutions available. But in the past four years, while focusing on trying to make the Internet safe for children, I unfortunately have seen tragedies and heard parents' horror stories. Shedding light on the worst of the Internet helps parents understand the necessity of monitoring their children online and implementing the safety tools that are available.

Like Susan, the parent at the beginning of this chapter, you may be fascinated yet troubled about the use of computers and the Internet. You may feel overwhelmed already by the sheer amount of information in this chapter. After reading about the risks, you may even be considering unplugging your computer from the Internet.

But rather than raising computer- and Internet-illiterate children, you can implement responsible safeguards, ensuring that your children will have safe, educational, and entertaining online experiences. Educate yourself about cyberspace. Raise your awareness of the benefits as well as the risks of going online. Take advantage of the safety tips and information on software tools and technology in these pages. Just by reading this book, you have accepted the challenge of making your child's trek in cyberspace a safe experience.

The decisions you make as a parent today will influence your child's destiny. And the steps you take as an advocate for other children will help shape the cyberspace community while it is still in its formative stages. You and I have the unique opportunity to shape this new interactive media environment so that it becomes a positive force in the lives of our children and grandchildren.

2

For Net-Shy Parents— Internet 101

"Eeek! It's a mouse!" Lily squealed with delight as she pulled a gray, oval device out of the computer packaging.

Susan let out a little scream.

"It's not that kind of mouse, Mom!" Lily responded in an annoyed tone. "This is what you use to point and click."

"Point and click what?" asked Susan.

"On the computer. You point and click on whatever you want to open," responded Lily. "Like a game. You just double click on the icon and the game opens."

"You're going to have to show me how to work this thing, Lily." Secretly, Susan wished Lily had wanted a real mouse instead of this computer equipment. *I would at least know what to do with a real mouse,* Susan thought as she held the computer mouse in her hand. *I feel so ignorant when it comes to this hardware!*

Susan followed the instructions, plugged the mouse into the computer, and pressed the power button. The machine whirred as various objects appeared on the screen.

"Look, Mom, it's working!" said Lily as she squeezed into the chair next to Susan.

"Okay, Lily, show me how to work this little contraption."

"It's easy, Mom," Lily said confidently. She placed her hand on the mouse and the cursor on the screen began to move.

"Now you try it."

Susan's hand felt awkward as she kept sliding the mouse off the mouse pad.

"This mouse pad is too small," Susan remarked.

"No it isn't," Lily responded. "When you get to the end of the pad, pick up the mouse and move it back. It's kind of like brushing hair. You use strokes."

Susan tried Lily's suggestion and watched the cursor jerkily move across the screen.

"It just takes practice," Lily assured her. "You'll catch on in no time."

Learning anything new takes time.[1] And for parents to become computer literate, they may need to look to their own children, as Susan did. I want to emphasize the importance of getting a handle on the basics. Unless you understand the foundational elements that are brought together by the Internet, you may find yourself wandering in a cybermaze, not knowing where you are and certainly unable to protect your child online.

The Basics of Hardware and Software

To get online, you need a computer with certain *hardware* (equipment) and *software* (instruction programs that can be installed on the computer) as well as online access. Internet essentials include:

- A computer with a monitor (screen), a keyboard for typing text and numbers on the screen, and a *mouse* (a small hand-controlled device for pointing and clicking to make selections on the screen). You may also want a printer, which will allow you to get hard copies (on paper) of what you see on the screen.

- A modem (either inside your computer or a separate piece of equipment outside) to allow your computer to communicate with other computers through the phone line. Communications software works with the modem to give the computer instructions for connecting to the Internet.

- A connection to the Internet through either an *Internet Service Provider (ISP)* or an *Online Service.* An ISP offers connection to the Internet; an online service connects you to the Internet and provides additional services. More on these services later.

- Software for using the Internet (may already be provided on your computer or through the Internet connection). To move around on the Web, you'll need Web *browser* software, such as Netscape Navigator, Communicator, or Microsoft Internet Explorer. You'll also need software such as Eudora, Netscape Mail, or cc:Mail for sending and receiving electronic mail. Browser, e-mail, and other software are often provided by the ISP or Online Service.

How Do I Choose a Computer?

You can get guidance about buying a computer from many sources:

- Consumer guides, computer magazines, and books available at your local library or bookstore
- Family members, friends, coworkers, and computer experts at your child's school or at your workplace
- Workshops or classes sponsored by community colleges, libraries, and computer stores
- Computer user groups
- Sales representatives or consultants at reputable computer stores

Become familiar with the following computer features so that you can make an informed decision:

- The size of the memory is measured in megabytes (MBs) or RAM (random access memory).
- The speed of the computer processor is measured in megahertz (MHz).
- The size of the computer's hard drive is measured in megabytes or gigabytes (GBs).
- The speed of the computer's modem is measured in kilobytes per second (KBs).

Internet Service Provider or Online Service?

An Internet Service Provider (ISP) provides you with the software you need to get on the Internet. ISPs include local and regional companies, nationwide providers such as UUNet and Netcom, and telecommunications companies such as AT&T and MCI. If your family is ready to explore the Internet independently, an ISP can be a wise choice. While most ISPs are lower in price, they also typically require more time, patience, and experience to learn to use effectively.

Online Services, such as America Online (AOL), Erols, Mayberry USA, and Microsoft Network (MSN), offer members Internet access along with a number of additional resources, which may include travel planning, financial management services, children's areas, and chat rooms, to name a few. Although many of the resources available through online services can also be found on the Internet, online services organize them attractively and make them easy for you and your children to access with the click of a mouse. Within their own resource areas, online services can also exercise more control over what their members see and do by blocking access to certain sites, providing parental controls, offering pornography-free service, and monitoring communication, particularly in children's areas.

Before you choose between an ISP and an online service, check out the costs and whether technical support is available. Many of these services offer free trial periods so that you can shop and choose what fits you best. Some, like AOL, offer a "bring your own access" price. You get the Internet from an ISP and then use it to access a cut-rate AOL. You'll also want to get information about parental controls and porn-free service.

Remember that while you're online, your modem will be using your phone line. You won't be able to make or receive any telephone calls until you disconnect from the Internet, unless you have a separate phone line for your modem.

What If I Can't Afford a Computer?

It's not necessary to own a computer to begin exploring the Internet. You may be able to get online by using the free facilities in your community.

A word of caution: Since many public Internet terminals are not equipped with protective software (blocking/filters), parents must pay particular attention to the information and precautions discussed in this book to avoid exposure of children to pornography and other online dangers.

Places to try:

- A public institution such as a library or community center. Some public housing complexes have a computer center with free online access for their residents.
- Your child's school or a community college or university where you are taking a class.
- Your employer, who may encourage you to learn new online skills by using company computer equipment for a limited amount of time each day.
- Your local shopping mall, which may have a room with computers for use by those visiting the mall.

Some communities sponsor *freenets* to give all their members free access to a wealth of information. To see if there is a freenet in your area, have someone with Web access go to http://www.lights.com/freenet/.

Beginning the Journey

When you go on the Internet, you may have a specific destination in mind or you may wish to browse the Web as you would a catalog or directory, looking for things that interest you. This browsing is called *surfing the Net* or *cruising the Information Superhighway.* There are several ways to get around on the Web.

Web Addresses

To get to a specific destination, you type in an Internet address in the space provided on the Web browser. Web addresses, sometimes called *Uniform Resource Locators (URLs)* begin with http://, which stands for *HyperText Transfer Protocol.* After you type in the Web address, it may take a while for the site's *home page* to appear on the screen, especially if it includes many pictures. Once it does, you'll probably see several choices on which you can click your mouse to take you further into the site.

How Can I Assist My Child in Finding Appropriate Content Online?

Here are a few resources to get you started. Also check out appendix A: Resources for Kids and Parents.

Enough Is Enough
http://www.enough.org
Net-mom
http://www.netmom.com
The Internet Kids & Family Yellow Pages
(Osborne/McGraw-Hill, 1997) by Jean Armour Polly
(Net-mom™)
The Children's Partnership
http://www.childrenspartnership.org
Disney's Family.com
http://www.family.com

▶ **Family Education Network**
  http://familyeducation.com
  Internet Online Summit: Focus on Children
  http://www.kidsonline.org
  Parent Soup
  http://www.parentsoup.com
  SafeSurf
  http://www.safesurf.com
  Time Warner Inc.
  http://www.pathfinder.com
  http://www.parenttime.com
  http://www.kids.warnerbros.com
  http://cartoonnetwork.com

Hypertext Links

Many sites include *hypertext links (hot links)* to other
sites with related content. When you click on one of the
highlighted areas, your computer will connect to another
Web site without your having to know or type its address.

Search Engines

Search engines are programs that you can select from
your Web browser to enable you to search the Internet
by keywords or topics. They usually show up on the computer screen through your browser. For example, if you
want to find out more about basketball player Michael
Jordan, you can click on a search engine, enter his name,
then pull up several Web sites for further exploration.
    Examples of search engines include:

• AltaVista—http://www.altavista.digital.com
• Infoseek—http://www.infoseek.com

- Lycos—http://www.lycos.com
- Magellan—http://www.magellan.com
- N2H2—http://www.n2h2.com
- Webcrawler—http://www.webcrawler.com
- Yahoo—http://www.yahoo.com
- Yahooligans! (for children)—http://www.yahooligans.com

You can find these search engines and many more at the All-in-One site: http://www.albany.net/allinone/ or your Web browser's home page.

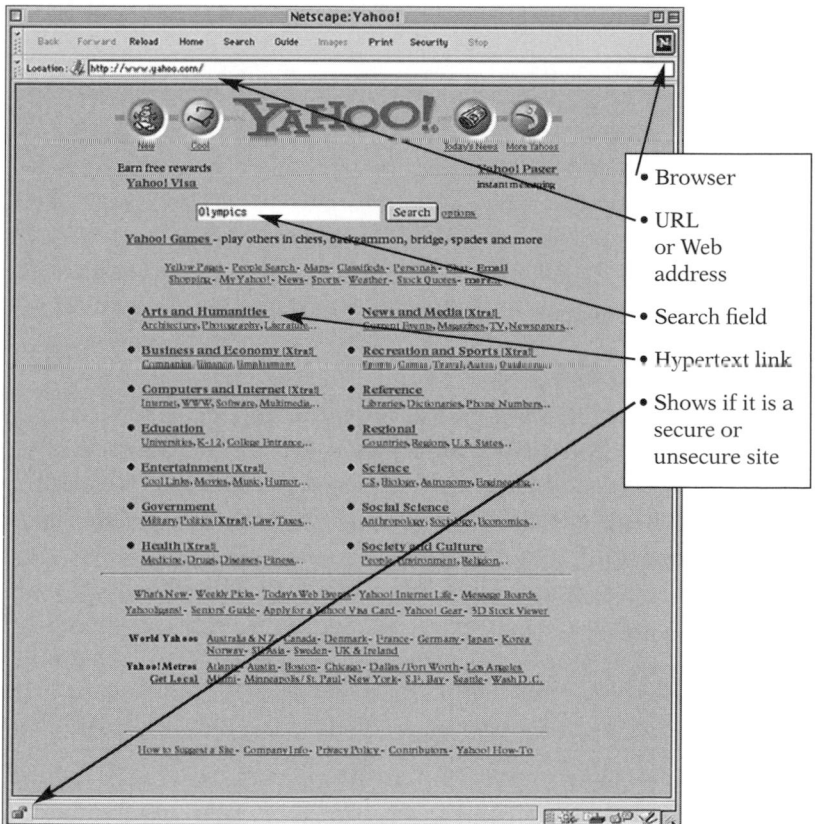

Bookmarks

As you look through the Internet, you'll find sites you want to revisit. You can create a *bookmark* by saving the address on your computer, usually with just a click of the mouse. The help feature on your Web browser can give you specific instructions. When you want to return to the site, you just click its address on your list of favorite sites.

Saving Information from the Internet

As you surf the net and come across information that you want to keep, you can either print a hard copy directly from the Web, or you can *download* a copy of the information onto your own computer.

Printing

Click on the print command or *icon* or click on FILE, then click on PRINT. The printer connected to your computer will print a copy. Or you may want to use the mouse to highlight only the information you would like to print.

Downloading

To use the information you discover on the Internet on your own computer, use your mouse to click on a command or icon to download it (often FILE, then SAVE AS). Be aware that when you download files from the Internet, you can bring back *viruses*, or programs, that can destroy your personal files and software. For protection, buy—and regularly update—an antivirus program.

Electronic Communication

One of the most popular online activities is communicating with individuals and groups through e-mail, *listserv* discussion groups, and USENET newsgroups.

E-mail

You and your child will probably be sending notes and even pictures to friends and family. To send them an e-mail message, you need their e-mail address. E-mail addresses usually start with a version of the person's name (or screen name) and continue with the "at" sign (@), the ISP's name (usually abbreviated), a period (called "dot"), and a three-letter extension, such as com or edu. Make sure that when you type an address, you key it exactly as it is given to you—copy the capitalization, spacing, and punctuation. Some examples of e-mail addresses are:

- jdoe@cd.gov
- cbass@school.edu
- sgreene@nonprofit.org
- screenname@ISP.com

It's a good safety precaution to make up screen names and never use your real name in chat rooms, discussion groups, and other places on the Internet. This will make it difficult for strangers to contact you and other family members by phone, by e-mail, or in person.

CAUTION

Listservs

You and your child can use e-mail to participate in discussion groups focused on topics that interest you. When you subscribe to a listserv, you can read all the messages sent to members of the group. You can also send messages to the entire group. Each group has an administrator who sets the rules for how the group will operate. If the listserv is moderated, the administrator will also keep the discussion on track and make sure participants treat each other courteously, or follow *netiquette* (for more information on netiquette, see page 114). A list of listservs and the e-mail addresses for subscribing to them is available at http://www.lizst.com.

USENET Newsgroups

USENET is a private group of companies that maintain and distribute newsgroups from their servers to the ISPs. The ISPs subscribe to USENET and provide access to their customers. Unlike listservs, USENET newsgroups do not require users to subscribe.

USENET newsgroups are a popular part of online communications. They are similar to BBS message boards, allowing users to take part in communities of people interested in particular topics, such as reviews of books, software upgrades, recipes, and technical scientific discussions. The name of the newsgroup reflects its focus. Newsgroups registered with USENET form a system of thousands of special interest groups distributed through computers serving the Internet and provide forums for discussion of more than twenty thousand topics by millions of people worldwide. Users are able to post messages and pictures for anyone to see. And anyone can respond by posting a general message or sending an e-mail to the author of an earlier message.

Most newsgroups are unmoderated, meaning that every message and picture sent will automatically appear in that newsgroup. When a newsgroup is moderated, only messages that are approved by the newsgroup's administrator will be posted to the group. See chapter 3 for more information on USENET newsgroups.

> Most newsgroups are not moderated; no one keeps the discussion focused on the topic or exercises control over inappropriate or illegal behavior. Many topics are not suitable for children! Due to the amount of illegal content posted, such as child pornography and hard-core obscenity, parents would be unwise to allow their children to access USENET without protective screening software and/or close adult supervision.

 CAUTION

Beginner Safety Tips

We tell our children to be wary of strangers they meet, but we need to do more than just tell them to be cautious of strangers on the Internet. More thorough information on creating a safety net for your child and using appropriate technological solutions can be found in chapters 5, 6, and 7. But for now, I suggest that you immediately teach your children that they must:

- Never give out personal information or use a credit card online without your permission.
- Never share their *password,* even with friends.
- Never arrange a face-to-face meeting with someone they met online unless you are present.
- Never respond to messages that leave them feeling confused or uncomfortable. Encourage them to ignore the sender, end the communication, and tell you or another trusted adult immediately.
- Be cautious in assuming that the people they meet online are who they say they are.

Now that you know the basics, I want to encourage you to keep on reading and exploring the risks that your child faces when he or she goes online. I must warn you that many of the pornographic images and materials that are explained in the next few chapters may make you feel uncomfortable. I think that's probably a good sign!

Cybersavvy Quiz #1

Take the following quiz to see how cybersavvy you are. Then use the glossary to get more specific information on areas that are confusing or unclear.

1. The Internet is:
   a. a warehouse run by computer programmers
   b. a file of information stored in the phone lines
   c. a global network of computers that connects more than eighty-two million people in more than one hundred countries
2. The World Wide Web is:
   a. a massive, complex network of phone lines
   b. a catalog ordering house
   c. the popular multimedia part of the Internet where you can link to graphics, sound, video, other media, or documents
3. Internet Service Providers:
   a. help you repair fishing nets for your yacht
   b. help you determine how many phone lines you need inside your computer
   c. help you access the Internet for hourly or monthly fees
4. To send an e-mail message:
   a. you must always use the proper salutation
   b. you must keep it short and to the point

c. you must know the Internet address of the person you're sending e-mail to
5. A cookie is:
   a. what you'll find in a jar in the kitchen
   b. a computer term for good content
   c. a piece of information that may be stored in the browser of your computer

Scoring: If you chose answer C for every question, you answered correctly. Congratulations! If you missed several answers, take some time to reread this chapter and become more familiar with the terms as you work through this book and go online more often.

For further information on family use of the Internet, refer to the following resources. A complete list of resources is given in appendix A.

Internet Family Fun: The Parent's Guide to Safe Surfing, Bonnie Bruno with Joel Comm, http://www.worldvillage.com/familyfun/sites.htm

Parents Guide to the Internet, U.S. Department of Education

3

The Serious Risks of Cyberspace

Tentatively Susan leaned forward as she watched her new computer screen begin to change. She felt a little overwhelmed by all this information at her fingertips. She could still remember the long hours she spent at the library when she was Lily's age— looking through encyclopedias, trying to find books that had been checked out or were missing, thumbing through the hard-to-use card catalog, waiting in long lines to seek help from a reference librarian. Now that she and Tom had invested in a personal computer, their child would never suffer the same inconveniences they had experienced. Instead, with the click of a mouse, Lily could hear the actual cry of a wolf, visit the National Gallery of Art, enter an Easter egg painting contest, learn a foreign language, send e-mail messages to her friends, and more. The possibilities were endless. In fact ten-year-old Lily was putting the new computer to very good use.

"Mom, whatcha doin'?" Lily's voice brought Susan back to earth.

"I'm looking for a Web site on counseling."

"Did you type in the right letters?"

"I think so."

Lily leaned over her mom's shoulder and examined the screen.

"Mom, that doesn't look like a normal web address."

"Well, it must be right; it's in the counseling organization's newsletter."

Lily watched over Susan's shoulder as words appeared on the screen:

```
For photos, press enter or click mouse
on continue.
```

Susan pressed the enter key and turned to stroke Lily's hair.

"Go get your brush, and I'll see if I can get those tangles out."

"No-o-o, it'll hurt!" whined Lily.

"I'll be careful. Go get your brush."

Lily slowly shuffled toward her bedroom as Susan turned back to the screen. The scene that met her eyes caused her to gasp for air as her heart pounded. She could hear Lily singing to herself as she returned with her brush.

Susan fumbled for the mouse, clicking wildly, trying to remove the nude photo from the computer screen. *How could this happen? What have I done?*

Thinking quickly, she remembered she could turn off the power to the monitor. The screen went dark.

She shuffled through the mail on her desk and found the counseling newsletter that had come in the mail last week. There in bold letters was the address.

Oh no! I typed in .com instead of .org! Susan felt embarrassed. *Just one little mistake and look where it took me!*

Parents, institutions, and governments have never allowed minors to have unrestricted access to pornography on magazine racks, cable channels, satellite TV, or dial-a-porn. But now, through the Internet, many children, with few restrictions, are able to easily access for free both soft-core and hard-core pornography in their own homes. Defending minor children from harmful pornography goes beyond questions regarding censorship to how society should behave responsibly in protecting children from material that victimizes them.

As I mentioned in the introduction, as a parent and an advocate for children, I have two major concerns about child safety on the Internet:

- When children go online, they have easy access to every type of pornography conceivable.
- The Internet makes it possible for pedophiles and sexual predators to have easy access to children.

As I've spoken and listened to people across the country and around the world, there is general consensus that pornography, particularly illegal pornography, can have devastating effects on our children. Most parents are concerned about their children talking to strangers or playing alone on the playground, but how many nonchalantly allow their children to interact on the Internet—at home, at school, or at the library—without guidance and supervision?

Like the real world, the virtual cyberworld contains sex, violence, and other content that is dangerous and inappropriate for our children. While hazardous material also exists beyond the Internet, the unregulated nature of the Internet makes it more difficult to keep illegal and harmful material out of the hands of our children.

For our children to safely develop their potential online, we need to address the destructive misuse of this technology. Keep in mind that the technology itself is neutral; it's the exploitation of this new technology that poses threats to our children. This chapter will help you to further understand the risks of going online and how you can begin to respond to the dangers.

Online Pornography

Computers have emerged as the leading-edge technology for the distribution of pornography. This is due to the lower risk of law enforcement detection, speed of transmission, and ease of access for both children and adults. In fact the Internet has become the primary channel for distributing child pornography worldwide.

Some of the highest traffic on the Web is to pornography sites. Just look at the following reports:

- According to the *Washington Post,* adult sites generate an estimated one billion dollars in revenue yearly.[1]
- The *Playboy* Web site has received 4.7 million hits in one seven-day period.[2]
- "Adult" entertainment on the Internet is the third largest sector of sales, surpassed only by computer products and travel.[3]

- Blocking software vendors report that there are between 72,000 and 100,000 sexually explicit pornographic sites on the Internet.[4]
- Most ISPs provide public access to hundreds of USENET newsgroups that are specifically reserved for posting explicit and extreme categories of pornography (i.e., alt.sex.snuff.cannibalism, alt.sex .bestiality, alt.binaries.pictures.erotica.teens, etc.). All these are as freely accessible to an intrepid ten year old as to an adult.[5]
- A new Web site appears every twenty-two seconds—more than thirty-nine hundred new sites every day. Today at least eighty-five of those new sites will be selling commercial pornography.[6]
- In its project "Innocent Images," FBI personnel acknowledged in 1997 that the Bureau has a database of at least four thousand cases of child pornography being distributed online.[7]
- In 1995 police arrested Robert Thomas, a pornographer operating an international computer *bulletin board service (BBS)* called "Amateur Action." They seized more than five thousand images featuring the exhibition of child genitals in addition to violent, bestial, hebephiliac, coprophiliac, and other forms of hard-core pornography. Computer analysts confirmed that these images had been downloaded in more than two thousand cities around the world.[8]

Types of Pornography

Pornography can be thought of as all sexually explicit material intended primarily to arouse the reader, viewer, or listener. Each category of illegal pornography has a specific legal definition established by the courts. See also appendix D for the legal definitions of types of pornography.

The Supreme Court has said that there are four categories of pornography that can be determined illegal. Illegal pornography includes indecency, material harmful to minors, obscenity, and child pornography.

Indecency

Indecent material includes messages or pictures on telephone, radio, or broadcast TV that are patently offensive descriptions or depictions of sexual or excretory organs or activities. This is often referred to as "sexual nudity" and "dirty words."

Material Harmful to Minors

Material harmful to minors represents nudity or sex that has prurient appeal for minors, is offensive and unsuitable for minors, and lacks serious value for minors. This material is often referred to as soft-core pornography. There are "harmful to minors" laws in every state.

Note: Indecent and harmful to minors material is legal for adults but illegal when knowingly sold or exhibited to minors (children under the age of eighteen). There is currently no federal indecency or harmful to minors statute that applies to the Internet. (See legislative update on page 57.)

Obscenity

Obscenity is graphic material that is obsessed with sex and/or sexual violence and is, therefore, prurient, patently offensive, and lacking in serious value. It is often referred to as hard-core pornography and includes close-ups of graphic sex acts and deviant activities, such as penetration, group sex, bestiality, torture, incest, and excretory functions. There are federal obscenity laws that criminalize distribution of obscenity on the Internet, but they have not been vigorously enforced.

Child Pornography

Child pornography is material that visually depicts children (real children as well as computer-generated depictions of children) under the age of eighteen engaged in actual or simulated sexual activity, including lewd exhibition of the genitals. Child pornography laws were recently amended to include computerized images or altered *(morphed)* pictures of children, and counterfeit or synthetic images generated by computer that appear to be of real minors or that were marketed or represented to be real child pornography. Laws dealing with child pornography on the Internet are being enforced, but the problem appears to be larger than state or federal law enforcement can control.

You may have trouble distinguishing between the types of pornography. Or you may be wondering why some pornography is on the Internet if it's illegal. For answers to these questions as well as more information on how we can legally protect children from pornography without infringing on the free speech rights of adults, check out appendix D: Pornography on the Internet.

> In 1997, after the U.S. Supreme Court ruled that the indecency provisions of the Communications Decency Act were unconstitutional, *Penthouse* posted the following on their Web site: "the Supreme Court struck a blow for Liberty, and cleared the

way for *Penthouse* to build the Ultimate Empire of Sex on the Internet."[9]

In response to the ruling, the Children's Online Protection Act (S.R. 1482 and H.R. 3783) is before Congress as of June 1998. The bill would force commercial pornographers on the World Wide Web to require adult verification or use of a credit card for access to their Web site. This would end the commercial pornographers' practive of placing free "teaser" images on the home page of their Web sites, which children are now able to access as I've discussed in chapter 3. It will not protect children from accessing pornography via e-mail, chat rooms, Usenet newsgroups, or commercial Web sites operating outside of the United States. Therefore, even if this bill is signed into law, all of the safegaurds discussed in this book are still applicable and should be implemented to protect children from accessing pornography online. (See more on the Children's Online Protection Act in appendix D.)

Child Stalking Laws

The Communications Decency Act contains an important amendment to federal law to protect children from online pedophiles and stalkers. In addition, there are numerous other federal and state criminal laws in place to prosecute Internet-facilitated sexual contact with minors.

How Children Access Pornography on the Internet

When I first discovered what types of pornography are being generated on the Internet, I was alarmed. But when I actually saw the disgusting material available on the Internet to any child who stumbles across it, I was truly repulsed and saddened. In some instances a child can click on picture files, and images appear on the computer screen free of charge. Any computer-literate child can view adult pornography, such as images that appear in *Playboy* or *Penthouse,* as well as pornography that is prosecutable as obscenity, which might include pictures of women having sex with dogs, horses, and snakes; men engaged in sexual acts with children; and the rape, torture, and mutilation of women.

Children can access such pornography in two ways: unintentionally and intentionally.

Unintentional Access

A friend and former colleague, Doris Evans, shared her daughter's story with me. As a seventh grader, her daughter was writing a book report on *Little Women* when she decided to do some research on the Internet. When she typed the words *little women* into the search engine on her computer, she found more than information on Louisa May Alcott's classic. An X-rated entry that promised "Women! Women! Women!" appeared on her screen.

According to a 1997 GRIP student poll, 63 percent of the students had unintentionally downloaded pornography while surfing the Internet on their home computer. Like Doris's daughter, many children can inadvertently access pornography in several ways:

- *Innocent, imprecise, misdirected searches.* In an effort to increase traffic to their sites, pornographic Web site operators use popular terms. When children key in their favorite search terms, pornographic sites pop up along with the sites the chil-

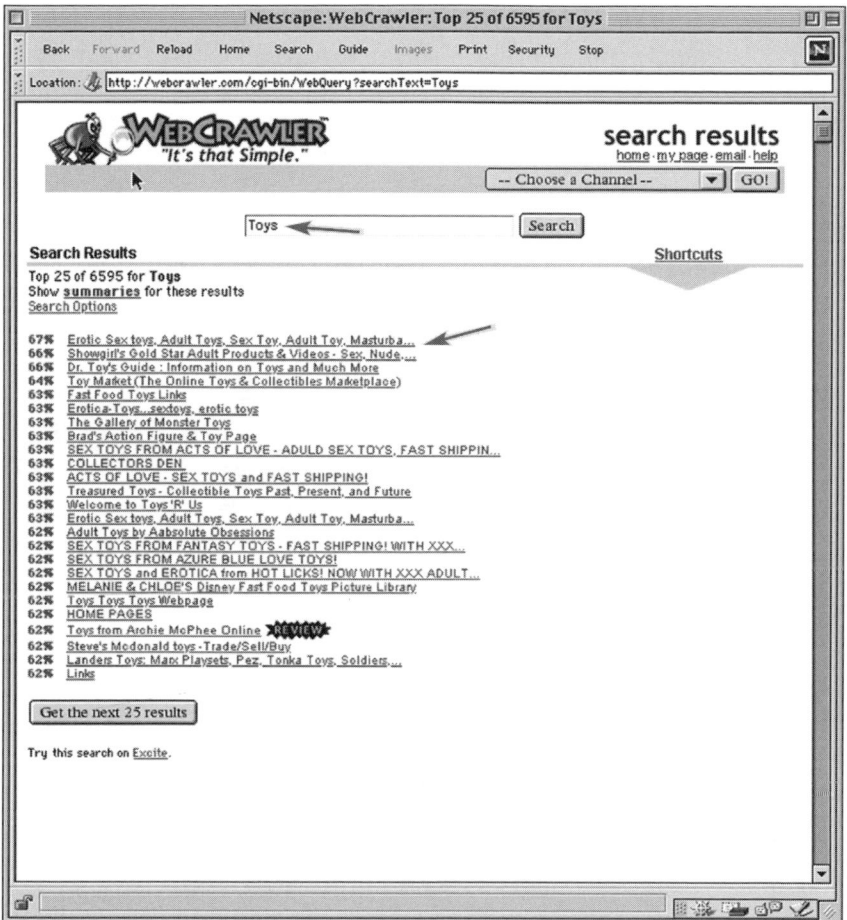

This is an unintentional search.

dren are seeking. The search engines don't distinguish between an adult's hit and a child's hit.

- *Mistaken, mistyped, or misleading URLs.* Many children seeking the Mars Mission photos found themselves confronted with a pornographic site and direct free links to hard-core pornography when they typed in NASA.com rather than NASA.gov. While that site has been shut down, it is not an isolated incident and other similar examples exist.

Domain Names

The last few letters in the *domain name* sometimes give clues to the location of the server as well as the type of organization represented. Sometimes the last two letters of the URL designate the country of origin. For example, a Web site with the suffix .us is probably in the United States, while one with .ca is in Canada. Others are not so obvious. For example, .za is South Africa and .va comes from The Holy See, the Vatican. In addition to these two-letter country codes, three-letter top level domain names (TLDs) are also used. Current common TLDs include:

- .gov or .mil—indicates a government or military site, such as the White House: www.whitehouse.gov (but whitehouse.com is a pornography site)
- .com—indicates a business or commercial site, such as Disney's Daily Blast: www.disneyblast.com
- .edu—indicates an educational site, such as Cornell University: www.cornell.edu
- .org—indicates a nonprofit organization, such as Enough Is Enough: www.enough.org
- .net—indicates a network such as pacbell.net

- *The need to constantly say no.* A reporter shared with me how her nine-year-old son (who couldn't care less about girls or sex at his age) did a search for Beanie Babies. He found many links to Beanies, and "Hot Cyber Babes!!" also appeared in the list. If he had clicked on that link, her son would have been connected to that site and able to freely view pornographic pictures. Once he viewed the free pictures, the site would have required a credit card number and an *adult password*. Without saying no at least three times, he would have seen the free pictures and damage would have been done. The constant need to say no conflicts with a child's natural curiosity. If a child, out of curiosity or carelessness, clicks on such links, he or she may be exposed to material that can never be erased from the mind.

- *Unsolicited e-mail.* Unsolicited commercial e-mail (UCE) messages are referred to as *spam*. Spammers can get e-mail addresses in many ways and they send hundreds of thousands of pieces of junk e-mail every day. They try to boost traffic by advertising pornography for sale and "make-money-fast" schemes.

  In the case of pornographic spam, children open their e-mail and find direct access links to porno graphic sites. Many of these e-mails contain subject lines that are deceptive; for example, "Please Help Me." Who wouldn't open mail with that subject heading? Children and adults are unable to determine the mail's true contents until the mail is opened and read, and by that time the damage is done. In addition, some Web browsers automatically open to display images that may be pornographic. Also disturbing is the fact that a child can be automatically switched to an adult Web page—exhibiting sexually explicit images—without even clicking on the link!

- *Instant messages (IMs).* Children are also vulnerable to receiving pornographic content through private, real-time communication with sexual predators. In addition, when certain people think that their identities are somewhat anonymous and they have a captive audience, they take the opportunity to direct *flames* (abusive or vulgar messages) to others, including children.

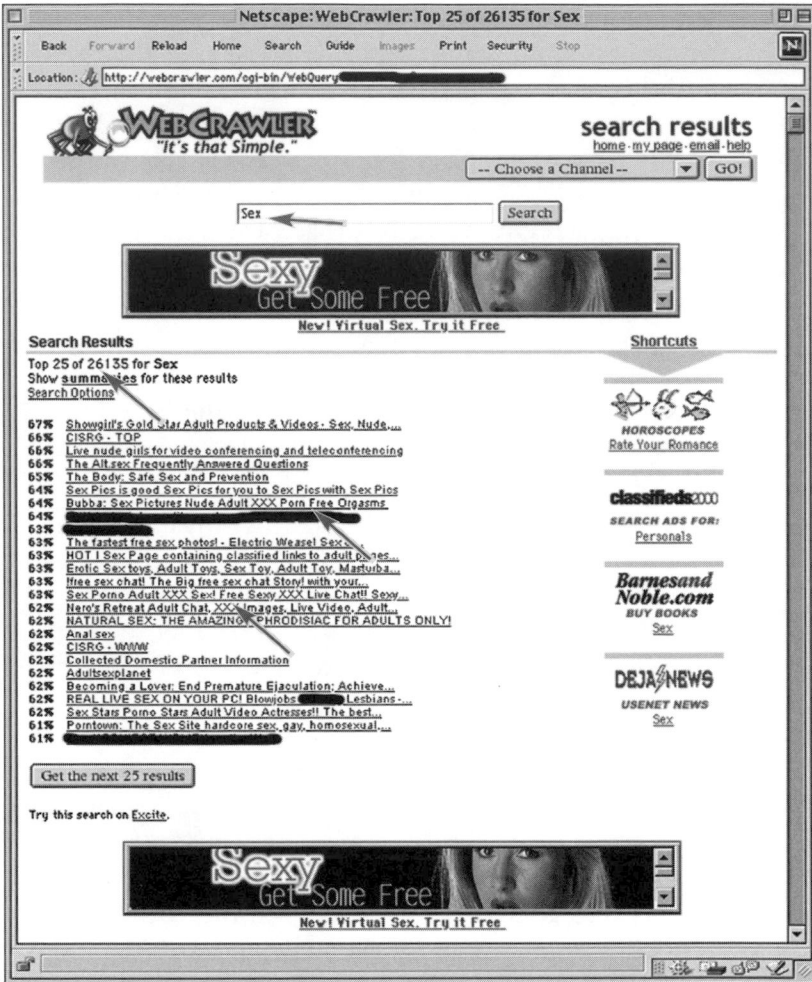

This is an intentional search

Intentional Access

Some of the very qualities that make the Internet so powerful and attractive—vast amounts of information easily navigated via powerful search engines—make it a "pornucopia."[10] Even the most diligent parental guidance and supervision sometimes do not deter a child who is determined to view pornography on the Internet. Eighty-one percent of the students responding to the GRIP poll admitted to intentionally downloading pornography on their home computer. Children have access to computers and the Internet not only at home, but in many other places—at school, libraries, or the home of a friend. Though *your* child may not directly access pornography, he or she may come into contact with other children who *are*, since online pornography is widely available to the public at large. In 1996 two fifteen-year-old boys in St. Petersburg, Florida, downloaded pictures of child pornography and bestiality (sex depicting humans and animals) from the Internet onto floppy disks and sold them at school for five dollars each.[11]

In the past, those who wanted to view hard-core pornography, particularly that which might be prosecutable, had to overcome the embarrassment of others watching them enter an adult bookstore or peep show. Obviously it was very difficult for children to see hard-core pornography with these limitations. Even soft-core "men's" magazines are not sold to minors or displayed so minors can see them.

With the advent of online pornography, however, there has been a boom in new and younger pornography users. According to one survey, 81 percent of the students surveyed have intentionally downloaded pornography while surfing the Internet from their home connection, 18 percent from their school connection, and 11 percent from a public library connection.[12] Since adolescent males make up one of the largest consumer groups of pornography, and their access on the Internet is largely unrestricted, they may be facing an even more serious problem—sexual addiction. See chapter 4 for more on this problem.

Top Ten Words Used for Searching the Internet

1. free	6. XXX
2. sex	7. Diana
3. nude	8. pics
4. pictures	9. new
5. warez	10. university

Note that 30 percent of the search terms were directly related to pornography, and another 20 percent may be related to pornography.

From *Movieguide* (March 1998), 25; original source: *Washington Post Magazine* (26 October 1997).

The Nature and Location of Pornography on the Internet or through Online Services

Computer pornography is found primarily in the following areas:

Adult Bulletin Board Services (BBSs)

While Bulletin Board Services are not located on the Internet itself, BBS computers can be accessed through an Internet Service Provider. One law enforcement official has said, "There are computer bulletin boards set up specifically for the seduction of children. They lure kids in with games and establish relationships with them on-line. [Then] they arrange to meet face-to-face."[13]

One popular BBS provides more than twenty-five thousand picture files (featuring violence, excretory material, and hard-core pornography). In 1995 police seized

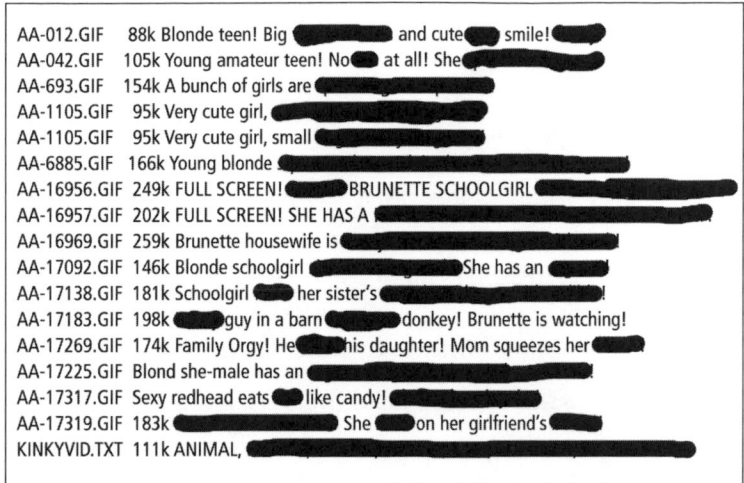

The words in this menu were so pornographic that we could not print them in our book, but this gives you an idea of what children can access. This is just a sample of the over 25,000 picture files available on the AA Bulletin Board Service. In 1995 police seized 5,000 images of children from this service. The number next to the "AA-" gives you an idea of the number of images available.

from this business more than five thousand images featuring the exhibition of child genitals.[14] These pictures are as clear and vivid as those found in magazines and videos. The full list of files comprises more than five hundred single-spaced, typed pages.

This particular BBS is owned by Robert Thomas, who is now in jail for distributing obscenity. Yet his BBS is still in operation! When Thomas was indicted in 1995, he had approximately three thousand subscribers. Computer analysts confirmed that the demand for the pedophiliac images exceeded availability by more than 25 percent. They also confirmed that these images had been downloaded in more than two thousand cities around the world.[15] While most pornographic BBSs are commercial, pictures from such services become available to children when

they surface in noncommercial areas, such as in USENET
newsgroups.

USENET Newsgroups

USENET newsgroups have become an anonymous
trading ground for illegal pornography. Material found
in the newsgroups is typically free of charge since
USENET newsgroups are provided by your ISP as part
of your Internet and online bundle of services. USENET,

```
13945 groups

alt.binaries.pictures.erotica
alt.binaries.pictures.erotica.amateur.d
alt.binaries.pictures.erotica.amateur.female
alt.binaries.pictures.erotica.amateur.male
alt.binaries.pictures.erotica.anime
alt.binaries.pictures.erotica.autos
alt.binaries.pictures.erotica.bestiality
alt.binaries.pictures.erotica.bestiality.hamster.duct-tape
alt.binaries.pictures.erotica.bestiality.hamster.duct-tape.d
alt.binaries.pictures.erotica.black.females
alt.binaries.pictures.erotica.blondes
alt.binaries.pictures.erotica.bondage
alt.binaries.pictures.erotica.breasts
alt.binaries.pictures.erotica.cartoons
alt.binaries.pictures.erotica.children
alt.binaries.pictures.erotica.d
alt.binaries.pictures.erotica.female
alt.binaries.pictures.erotica.fetish
alt.binaries.pictures.erotica.furry
alt.binaries.pictures.erotica.gaymen
alt.binaries.pictures.erotica.latina
alt.binaries.pictures.erotica.male
alt.binaries.pictures.erotica.orientals
alt.binaries.pictures.erotica.pornstar
alt.binaries.pictures.erotica.pregnant
alt.binaries.pictures.erotica.spatch
alt.binaries.pictures.erotica.teen
alt.binaries.pictures.erotica.teen.d
alt.binaries.pictures.fine-art.d
alt.binaries.pictures.fine-art.digitized
alt.binaries.pictures.fine-art.graphics
alt.binaries.pictures.fractals
alt.binaries.pictures.furniture
alt.binaries.pictures.furry
alt.binaries.pictures.girlfriend
alt.binaries.pictures.girlfriends
```

like a BBS, is not technically part of the Internet itself. The illegal content on USENET has proliferated in two primary ways. First, due to the free advertising possibilities, commercial pornographers, operating on the Web or through a BBS, post in (or send messages to) USENET newsgroups to advertise their services and entice people to subscribe. Second, USENET newsgroups provide an avenue for those who have become addicted to certain types of pornography to upload their pornographic files in exchange for new material. Once a person becomes addicted, he or she keeps looking for more. Collectors of material worldwide post pornography on news groups, using the USENET to trade material back and forth. Most of the pornography on this part of the Internet can be found in two primary hierarchies: alt.sex and alt.binaries.pictures.erotica.

Notice the different groups available in the illustration on page 66. One click on any group will take your child into a listing of free picture files (picture files are denoted by jpg or gif) concerning the subject. The files consist of a combination of free pictures, requests for pictures, and messages. One click on the topics at the left will provide clear magazine/video-quality pictures that can be downloaded, printed, and passed on to others. If your child clicked on alt.binaries.pictures.erotica.children, the next series of pages to appear on the computer screen would include a request for images of children (see page 68).

AOL, Erols, Prodigy, and CompuServe have recently removed child pornography newsgroups from their own boards and systems. Subject to constitutional and statutory privacy safeguards, they have agreed to cooperate fully with law enforcement officials investigating child pornography on the Internet. As these service providers have become more aware that providing unrestricted access to all newsgroups (such as alt.sex.teens. or

```
┌─────────────────────────────────────────────────────────────────────────┐
│                    alt.binaries.pictures.erotica.children                 │
├─────────────────────────────────────────────────────────────────────────┤
│                              √ Circumcision (m/f)                         │
├─────────────────────────────────────────────────────────────────────────┤
│ From: ak94@cityscape.co.uk (The Cutter)                                   │
│ Organization: IP-GOLD User                                                │
│ Date: Wed, Jun 7, 1995 2:54:04 PM                                         │
│ Newsgroups: alt.binaries.pictures.erotica.children     Article 2 of 2 in thread │
├─────────────────────────────────────────────────────────────────────────┤
│ Hiya all, The Cutter is here...                                           │
│                                                                           │
│ For those with an interest in circumcision (male/female) check out the postings to │
│ alt.binaries.pictures.tasteless.                                          │
│ Enjoy and feedback to me.  Otherwise, just drop me a line!  Flames auto-trashed. │
│                                                                           │
│ I am also interested in pix of boys, any age but must be circumcised; girls 12-16. │
│                                                                           │
│ Snip, snip,                                                               │
│                                                                           │
├─────────────────────────────────────────────────────────────────────────┤
│       Peter Clark        Re: Hey Flamers                                  │
│   2   Swannie            SO CUTE index (f) - cute_idx.jpg (0/1)           │
│       Forest             Re: SO CUTE index (f) - cute_idx.jpg (0/1)       │
│   2 √ The Cutter         Circumcision (m/f)                               │
│       Larry R. Winfre…   Destroy Switzerland Now!                         │
│       Christopher Pet…   Re: Private traders wanted                       │
│       Shadow@Space       Test                                             │
├─────────────────────────────────────────────────────────────────────────┤
│        156   alt.binaries.pictures.erotica.female.anal                    │
│        412   alt.binaries.pictures.erotica.fetish                         │
│        190   alt.binaries.pictures.erotica.furry                          │
│        665   alt.binaries.pictures.erotica.gaymen                         │
│          2   alt.binaries.pictures.erotica.kwakiutl                       │
│        247   alt.binaries.pictures.erotica.latina                         │
│       4142   alt.binaries.pictures.erotica.male                           │
│         34   alt.binaries.pictures.erotica.male.anal                      │
│       2895   alt.binaries.pictures.erotica.orientals                      │
│        341   alt.binaries.pictures.erotica.pornstar                       │
└─────────────────────────────────────────────────────────────────────────┘
```

alt.sex.pedophilia) makes them potentially vulnerable to prosecution for possession of child pornography, they have begun eliminating newsgroups with potentially illegal content from their subscribers' access. ISPs and online services are not responsible for what happens out on the Internet and the Web, but they *are* responsible for what they know about within their own services and USENET access.[16]

While many of us would prefer that these providers also remove prosecutable obscenity from their services, this is an encouraging first step. The next step is to urge online services and ISPs to remove prosecutable (but not prosecuted!) obscenity from their systems.

Porn-free (filtered) services are possible and are now beginning to spring up, such as IllumaNet (illuma.net), Rated-G Online, FlashNet, and Mayberry USA.

World Wide Web

Many commercial porn Web sites ask, "Are you eighteen?" If a curious kid or teenager responds yes and clicks on the enter key, free teaser images often appear on the screen for sample viewing before a credit card number or adult password is requested. Few sites attempt to verify a user's age before providing free samples of their wares. Much of the pornography commercially available on the Web is of the hard-core variety, but nudity and soft-core pornography are available as well. More and more commercial Web sites are crossing the obscenity line by displaying PCV (penetration clearly visible). Adult sites specifically target their marketing, placing notices in USENET newsgroups while running ads and teasers that pop up on search directories such as Yahoo!

Danni Ashe, a former stripper and soft-core video actress, says she opened a commercial Web page, and her income immediately went to fifteen thousand dollars a month. That prompted her to add a premium membership service, giving users access to a library of nude photos and interviews with nude models for $9.94 a month. Now the pay site boasts seventeen thousand members, giving Ashe more than two million dollars in revenue in 1997. Judging from the e-mail she receives, she believes she is tapping a new market. "I think a lot of these guys have never even bought an adult magazine."[17]

Chat Rooms

Also popular and free on the Internet as well as on certain Online Service Providers' services are chat rooms where people can engage in real-time conversations. Chat rooms have become the playgrounds of the '90s and are used by pedophiles to contact children for illicit sexual encounters. The kinds of people who search for their victims through conversations with unsuspecting kids playing on the Internet have no limits or restrictions. Most dangerous are *Internet Relay Chats (IRCs)*, instant messages (IMs), and private and/or unmonitored chat rooms.

Video Conferences

With the advent of new video conferencing technology, people can go online and participate in video conferences from remote locales. Using this technology, adults can molest children while other adults watch. Some call it a "virtual molestation." This brings me to my second major concern about the Internet.

How Pedophiles and Cyberpredators Access Children on the Internet

A grand jury charged sixteen people in the United States and abroad with participating in a child porn ring, called the Orchid Club. At least two of these men were convicted. The members of this club had shared homemade pictures, recounted their sexual experiences with children, and chatted electronically over the Internet as two men forced a ten-year-old girl to pose in sexually explicit positions. The assailants videotaped the sexual abuse in real time, broadcasting it over the Internet so that other pedophiles could watch and make requests. Prosecutors said members of the group produced and traded child pornography, involving victims as young as five years old.[18]

After gaining the trust of a fourteen-year-old boy via computer, a cyberpredator arranged to meet him. Police say he shackled, tortured, and molested the boy. The boy's father later discovered that the two had been exchanging sexually explicit e-mail.

A fourteen-year-old New Jersey girl was lured into sending nude videos of herself to a forty-seven-year-old man, who had posed as a fifteen-year-old boy on the Net. Fortunately the girl's mother became aware of the situation, and at a meeting he had suggested, the man walked into the hands of the FBI. A fifteen-year-old California boy was not so lucky. No one was there to intervene when he agreed to meet an adult he met online. He was raped at their first meeting.

When a nineteen-year-old disabled student got a new computer in 1995, she thought a whole new world was about to open for her. Instead, a computer engineer used the Internet to lure her into meeting him at a local college, where he raped her. After striking up an online relationship with the young woman, who suffers from spina bifida, the engineer suggested that the pair meet to talk in person. They talked for a while in the school cafeteria; then the man wheeled his victim out to his van and forced her to have sex with him, despite her repeated resistance. After raping her, he left her at a bus stop.[19]

I could continue with horrendous stories of children and young women victimized by pedophiliac molesters—individuals who find gratification in becoming sexually involved with children or adolescents. We are right to be fearful of strangers who may connect with children in chat rooms and go from there to stalking or worse!

One of the attractions of the Internet is the anonymity of the user, and this is why it can be so dangerous. A child doesn't always know with whom he or she is interacting. Children may *think* they know, but unless it's a school friend or a relative, they really can't be sure. Often we think of pedophiles as having access to children out on the playground and other places, but because of the way the Internet works, children can actually be interacting on their home computers with adults who pretend to be children.

Child sexual exploitation occurs in every economic, social, ethnic, and religious group. With the explosion of the Internet into a powerful, worldwide medium, the danger to children, whether they are from New York or New Zealand, has drastically increased. Pedophiles and other sexual predators can use the Internet, with no precautions, to exchange names and addresses of other pedophiles and of potential child victims. Hidden behind screen names that are pseudonyms, they gather online and swap child pornography with amazing speed and in amounts beyond our wildest imagination, which excites them to molest even more.

Typically pedophiles operate in isolation and are, of necessity, antisocial. *Never before have pedophiles had the opportunity to communicate so freely and directly with each other.* Their communication on the Internet provides validation, or virtual validation, for their behavior. They share their conquests, real and imagined. They discuss ways to contact children, what works or doesn't work. They exchange tips on seduction techniques, how to lure children into their *own* nets.[20] They are using the technology of the Internet to train each other.

The increased Internet contact among pedophiles could undo the years of therapy and treatment of recovering pedophiles and threatens to unloose latent emotions in men and women who, no longer satisfied with child pornography, may set out in search of real victims.[21]

What Is Being Done to Prosecute Sexual Predators?

In 1993 the kidnapping of a Maryland boy led police and the FBI to two suspects who allegedly had used their computers to contact and sexually abuse several juveniles. Further investigations led the FBI to the discovery of wide

usage of the Internet by child pornographers and pedophiles. This discovery prompted the FBI to launch the
Innocent Images initiative with the help of the Child Exploitation and Obscenity Section of the Justice Department's Criminal Division. This undercover operation attempts to identify and develop criminal cases against
people who use the Internet to recruit minors for sex or
distribute child pornography. By the end of 1997 Innocent
Images had produced more than eighty convictions.[22]

To Report Illegal Online Activity

The National Center for Missing and Exploited Children (NCMEC) provides excellent resources concerning
sexual exploitation of children and related issues for the
lay public, counseling community, and law enforcement
agencies. NCMEC has created an extensive web presence
for its Exploited Child Unit: http://www.missingkids.com.
These web pages provide background information on
laws and legislation, tips and pointers for parents and
children, and lists of preventive resources on the various
aspects of child sexual exploitation.

In addition to its Web pages, NCMEC, in partnership
with the U.S. Postal Inspection Service, U.S. Customs
Service, and the Federal Bureau of Investigation, serves
as the National CyberTipline. To report possible illegal
online activity related to child pornography, predation,
or any other type of child sexual exploitation, call the
CyberTipline: 800-843-5678 (800-TheLost) or contact
their Web site: http://www.missingkids.com/cybertip.

The CyberTipline will refer your reported information as a lead to the FBI, U.S. Customs, and the U.S.
Postal Inspectors. The information will also be for-
warded locally when a specific local agency can be identified. If you or your child are in immediate danger, con-

tact your local law enforcement before reporting to the CyberTipline. Your first step is always to exit the computer—then make the call!

There are also private groups that are dedicated to protecting children online and that report crime to law enforcement officials. One such group is Cyber Angels (www.cyberangels.org).

After reviewing this chapter and looking at the huge burden placed on us as parents and advocates for children, your first reaction may be similar to mine: *This is more than I can handle!*

To meet the challenge, we need to be educated and to become more familiar with Internet uses and risks. We also need and deserve the joint commitment and creative support of the Internet industry, responsible corporations, community groups, schools, libraries, and law enforcement agencies.

The following chapters will help you in your role as a parent to do your part with your own children. You don't have to shoulder the burden by yourself. This is a shared burden. You are not alone!

Cybersavvy Quiz #2

Take the following quiz to see how cybersavvy you are. Then review this chapter and/or use the glossary to get more specific information on areas that are confusing or unclear.

1. On the Internet, pornography can be found:
   a. in e-mail
   b. on Web sites
   c. in USENET discussion groups
   d. all of the above

2. Choose the true statement:
   a. Soft-core and hard-core pornography can be found on the Internet.
   b. Pornography is one of the most profitable businesses on the Internet.
   c. Pornography can be defined as sexually explicit material intended primarily to arouse the reader, viewer, or listener.
   d. all of the above
3. While online, pedophiles may be able to contact your child:
   a. through instant messages (IMs)
   b. in chat rooms
   c. through unsolicited e-mail messages
   d. all of the above
4. A pedophile is someone who:
   a. has a sexual appetite for children
   b. views children as sex objects
   c. may or may not act out sexual desires with a child
   d. all of the above

Scoring: If you chose answer D for every question, you answered correctly. Congratulations! If you missed several answers, take some time to reread this chapter and become more familiar with the complicated issues surrounding online pornography and sexual predators.

For further information on the risks of cyberspace, refer to the following resources and see appendixes A and D.

The Take Action Manual, Enough Is Enough
Kinsey: Crimes and Consequences, Judith A. Reisman

4

Shedding Light on the Darkness of Pornography

Susan added tomatoes to the eighteen-bean soup she was stirring on the stove.

"Mom, can I go online and check my e-mail?" Lily yelled from the family room.

"Sure, Lily," Susan called back. "Just don't respond to any instant messages or chat stuff while you're on."

Susan could hear the modem dialing up the number for Internet access. As she stirred the soup, she recalled the nude photo that had appeared on her computer screen when she had typed an incorrect Web site address. *Maybe I should check on Lily. I'd rather tell her about sex myself than have her learn about it while she's online.*

Susan left the soup simmering and walked into the family room.

Lily sat in front of the screen, waiting for the Internet connection to complete itself.

The automated voice on their online service announced, "You have mail!" Susan watched as Lily clicked on the mail icon.

A list of e-mail messages appeared.

"Hey, I got a message from Dad!"

"Great. See if he says what time his flight is arriving back home tomorrow."

Susan read Tom's message over Lily's shoulder.

"Mom, I don't know who this message is from."

"Hmm?" Susan replied, as she tried to calculate how she could get Lily to her piano lesson at 4:30 P.M. and still pick up Tom at the airport at 5:00 P.M. *Maybe I can reschedule Lily's lesson. Or Tom could just catch a shuttle and I can pick him up at the bus stop.*

"Hey, Mom, somebody sent me some bad words and a picture!" Lily exclaimed.

Susan turned her attention to the screen and was horrified and angered at what her daughter was looking at. *Why would someone send her daughter such a pornographic message and that degrading photo?* Even more disturbing was the sender's request for Lily to scan in and send her picture in reply. Susan turned her attention to Lily, who was staring intently with wide eyes at the screen.

"Lily, this is not something I want you reading or looking at," Susan said quietly, hoping panic was not evident in her voice. "Delete it, honey, log off, and let's talk about what we saw. Okay?"

Depending on the explicitness of the material, children like Lily can be seriously traumatized when they are confronted with sexually graphic speech and/or photos. Like Susan, most adults recognize that exposing children to pornography is harmful. It gives them their first messages about sex without adult supervision or moral guidance. There are some adults, however—whom I have debated in various media interviews—who say they think showing pornography to kids is okay (Bob Guccioni, publisher of *Penthouse* magazine, is one of these).

Advocates of pornography encourage and promote many myths in defense of pornography. Public indifference to pornography is frequently rooted in ignorance of the facts. While some experts who deny harm are unaware of new research and studies that suggest health hazards, others repeat their denials as a matter of their personal politics and values. In this chapter you will find more research notes, studies, and statistics than in other chapters, because I want to bring to light credible evidence that will dispel the myths of pornography, particularly the myth that pornography is a victimless crime.[1] Tragically, even with solid evidence, controversy remains over the extent of pornography's harm to children.

The Myths of Pornography

Myth #1—Obscenity Is a Matter of Opinion

Many people argue that obscenity cannot be defined, that it is a matter of opinion. However, in the Supreme Court case of *Miller v California,* a clear, concise definition of obscenity is given. In layperson's terms, obscenity includes graphic material that contains recurring sexual activity and/or sexual violence that is unmistakably offensive and lacking in serious value.

Myth #2—Obscenity Is Protected by the First Amendment

The First Amendment gives us freedom of speech and protects our right to express ourselves freely. Unfortunately there are those who have perverted this freedom to meet their own self-serving needs and the sexual appetites of consumers. For more than forty years, however, the Supreme Court has held that obscenity is "outside the protection intended for speech and press at the time during which the First Amendment was written" *(Roth v U.S.,* 354 U.S. 476). People caught in this myth have overlooked the fact that the First Amendment does not protect slander, false advertising, perjury, *child pornography,* or *obscenity.*

Myth #3—Pornography Is Harmless Entertainment

Some people actually believe that pornography has little or no effect on those who view it. However, research studies show that pornography has the potential to harm individuals and our culture. We'll take a closer look at some of these harms and their implications for children later on in this chapter.

Myth #4—Pornography Reduces Dangerous Impulses

A great deal of evidence suggests that repeated exposure to pornography leads to the probability of acting out sexually rather than reducing dangerous impulses. Even when addiction to pornography does not lead to the commitment of serious sex crimes, it cannot be considered a *harmless* outlet for dangerous impulses. The viewing of pornography often creates a sexual appetite that is self-perpetuating and addictive. Apparently when undeterred, pornography consumers may become bored with one type of pornography and move on to even more explicit or deviant material.

Myth #5—If Legalized, Pornography Will Be Less in Demand and Sex Crimes Will Decrease

Throughout history, people have suggested that the legalization of contraband (such as alcohol and drugs) and certain activities (such as prostitution) will lower the demand for these substances and activities. On the contrary, experience tells us that this just isn't true. When the use of pornography is allowed to proliferate, the following tends to occur:

- Some users of pornography become addicted, demanding more explicit or deviant material.
- Child sexual abuse and rape rates have risen dramatically where existing pornography laws are not enforced.
- Red light districts continue to be havens for sex crimes.

An example of the opposite can be seen in Oklahoma. While rape increased in the remainder of the nation, a case study in Oklahoma reports a correlation between the vigorous enforcement of obscenity laws and a 27 percent decline in reported rapes over a six-year period.[2] This is a noteworthy reduction in the number of women and children who have experienced the horrors of rape.

Didn't sex crimes decrease in Denmark with pornography legalized? Apparently not. Some of the more serious types of sex crimes such as rape actually increased in number and rate following the legalization of pornography in Denmark.[3]

Myth #6—You Can't Legislate Morality

I hear this one a lot and I usually respond by trying to educate the speaker. *Every* piece of legislation here in the United States is based on some type of moral (often Judeo-Christian) conviction. For example, laws against murder and theft can be easily traced to the Ten Commandments ("Thou shall not kill," and "Thou shall not steal"). So we do use our laws in this country to legislate morality. And we need strong legislation to control illegal pornography and limit its impact on our children.

Myth #7—Viewing Pornography Is a Choice— Don't Buy It

Pornography is like a toxic gas. Those doing the polluting aren't necessarily the ones who are harmed by the pollution. Once the gas is released into the atmosphere, it is impossible to recapture and contain it. The pollution of pornography harms children, and we must work to protect our children from exposure in the online areas where they study and play. Besides, children and adults are being exposed to online pornography accidentally—it's not always their choice.

Myth #8—It's Not the Sex in Pornography That's the Problem; It's the Violence

Some people suggest that the violence in pornography is doing most of the harm—"Just eliminate the violence and the sex will be okay." Even if violence is eliminated, nonviolent pornography would include the following:

- child pornography
- incest-type pornography

- sex with animals
- group sex
- sex that humiliates and denigrates women and their sex role in male/female relationships
- obscene material that presents massive misinformation or distortions about human sexuality[4]

Our task as responsible parents and child advocates is to dispel these myths, particularly the concept that obscenity and child pornography are classified as rights of free expression. At the same time, we must also prepare to deal with the harmful effects of pornography on our society and the implications for all children.

How Pornography Harms Children

Before we look at the many ways pornography can be harmful, I want to assure you that every child who views pornography will not necessarily be affected and, at worst, traumatized in the same way. The effects of pornography are progressive and addictive for many people. Just as every person who takes a drink does not automatically become an alcoholic, every child who is exposed to pornography does not automatically become a sexual deviant or sex addict. However, since pornography has a new door to the home, school, and library through the Internet, it is important for us to look at the many ways that pornography can potentially harm our children.

Exposure to Pornography Threatens to Make Children Victims of Sexual Violence

As I mentioned in chapter 3, the Internet has proven a useful tool for pedophiles and sexual predators as they distribute child pornography, engage in sexually explicit conversations with children, and seek victims in chat rooms. The more pornography these individuals access, the higher the risk of their acting out what they see, including sexual assault, rape, and child molestation.

Alarming Facts

- One in three American girls and one in seven boys will be sexually molested by age eighteen (David Finkelhor, "Answers to Important Questions about the Scope and Nature of Child Sexual Abuse," 8).

- An average serial child molester has between 360 and 380 victims in his lifetime (Abel, et al., "Self-Reported Sex Crimes on Nonincarcerated Paraphiliacs," *Journal of Interpersonal Violence* 2, no. 1, [1987] 326).

- A primary consumer group of pornography is adolescent boys ages twelve to seventeen (Attorney General's Final Report on Pornography, 1986).

Pornography's Relationship to Rape and Sexual Violence

According to one study, early exposure (under fourteen years of age) to pornography is related to greater involvement in deviant sexual practice, particularly rape. Slightly more than one-third of the child molesters and rapists in this study claimed to have at least occasionally been incited to commit an offense by exposure to pornography. Among the child molesters incited, the study reported that 53 percent of them deliberately used the stimuli of pornography as they prepared to offend.[5]

The habitual consumption of pornography can result in a diminished satisfaction with mild forms of pornography and a correspondingly strong desire for more deviant and violent material. As we've seen, this material is now easily accessible online in newsgroups, free of charge.[6]

Pornography's Relationship to Child Molestation

In a study of convicted child molesters, 77 percent of those who molested boys and 87 percent of those who molested girls admitted to the habitual use of pornography in the commission of their crimes.[7] Besides stimulating the perpetrator, pornography facilitates child molestation in several ways. For example, pedophiles use pornographic photos to demonstrate to their victims what they want them to do. They also use them to arouse a child or to lower a child's inhibitions and communicate to the unsuspecting child that a particular sexual activity is okay: "This person is enjoying it; so will you."

Exposure to Pornography Frequently Results in Sexual Illnesses, Unplanned Pregnancies, and Sexual Addiction

As more and more children are exposed not only to soft-core pornography, but also to explicit deviant sexual material, they are learning an extremely dangerous message from pornographers: *Sex without responsibility is acceptable and desirable.* Because pornography encourages sexual expression without responsibility, it endangers children's health.

We live in a society that strives to erase differences between child and adult sexuality, where psychological and social contexts do not stress the differences between adults and children. One of the grimmer consequences of adult-like sexual activity among children has been a steady increase in the extent to which youth are afflicted with venereal disease.[8] In the United States about one in four sexually experienced teenagers acquires a sexually transmitted disease (STD) every year, resulting in three million cases of teenage STDs. Infectious syphilis rates have more than doubled among teenagers since the mid-1980s. More children contract sexually transmitted diseases each year than all the victims of polio in its eleven-year epidemic, 1942–1953.[9]

Another obvious result of children involved in adult sexual activity is the increased rate of pregnancy among teenagers. One million American teenage girls become pregnant each year.[10]

In addition to promoting unsafe sex, pornography creates in its consumer an appetite that is self-perpetuating and addictive.[11] Early emotional wounding is almost always a factor in pornography addiction. The following letter is just one example of the many letters I receive from adults who were introduced to pornography as children and are today struggling to overcome sexual addiction.

Dear Mrs. Hughes:

I can't believe I have fallen back this far. Why must I torture my body like this?

I am starting to borrow money again, enough to support my habit. I know the hopelessness of being a slave to addiction. I always return to alcohol because of this terrible guilt I feel inside. I was molested as a young boy and I just can't harbor this hate for him anymore. I grew up with a very distorted view of my sexual identity, which led to a life of bisexual behavior. I was also exposed to pornography at an early age, and have been fascinated with it ever since. Although my sexual addiction has remained at the level of voyeurism, I am terrified that it will progress into something unspeakable! Though I have not viewed any pornography for about a month, I still have 20 years' worth of images imbedded in my mind! At 34, this dual addiction has completely destroyed my life. It led to impotence and eventually a divorce from my beautiful wife.

I don't want to be this filthy person inside, and I don't want to live this way anymore. Can you help me?

T.

Research has shown that "males who are exposed to a great deal of erotica before the age of 14 are more sexually active and engage in more varied sexual behaviors as adults than is true for males not so exposed."[12] One study reveals that among 932 sex addicts, 90 percent of the men and 77 percent of the women reported that pornography was significant to their addiction.[13]

Exposure to Pornography Promotes Desensitization

Exposure to pornography can lessen our repulsion and our recognition of its potential harms.[14] As the Internet exposes us to a greater range and quantity of violent and deviant forms of pornography than ever before available, it is not unreasonable to suspect that our society could begin to accept the viciousness and immorality of rape. Children and adolescents, who are "educated" by early exposure to pornography, may more easily accept the idea of forced sex as reasonable and justified.[15] Societies that perceive force and violence as appropriate behaviors set the stage for child abuse and victimization.

The Sexual Addiction Trap

"Sexual communication among adults tends to decline in cultures in which pornography flourishes. So-called sex magazines turn out to be 'anti-sex' and the sexual activity in such a culture appears to go into decline. Print and movie pornography tend to trap males more often than females. It would be easy to believe that males are more visually oriented than females, but the evidence is less clear than we need to make that assertion. What we do know is that the male's hydraulic sex system and the exterior genitals keep him more aware of his sexual feelings than the typical female is. His ejaculation pattern, once begun, will continue, and his psychosocial sexual appetite tends to be fully developed within thirty-six months after that first ejaculation. The 'porn' market, therefore, exploits this normal development of male sexuality, with the tragic effect that addiction to pornography tends to desensitize the male, such that a bonded heterosexual relationship is not only unlikely to develop, but the genuine relationship with one exclusive person is not even desired."[16]

Exposure to Pornography May Incite Children to Act Out Sexually against Other Children

When Dianne Smith (not her real name) and her family moved to a sleepy little town in northeast Arizona, she felt confident that it would be a peaceful and safe community in which to raise her children. That serene life was interrupted when Dianne discovered that her three-year-old daughter, Tiffany, had been sexually molested and raped by a twelve-year-old boy Dianne had hired to watch Tiffany while she worked at her home-based business. She had been home while they played together. Dianne wondered how a twelve-year-old boy could come up with the atrocities he had committed. The boy's counselor eventually revealed that during a crucial time in the boy's life—when his parents were experiencing marital problems—the boy had been introduced to hard-core pornography at a summer camp. It was only a matter of time before the boy acted out what he had seen.[17]

Children often imitate what they've seen, read, or heard. Studies suggest that exposure to pornography can prompt kids to act out sexually against younger, smaller, and more vulnerable children. Experts in the field of childhood sexual abuse report that any premature sexual activity in children always suggests two possible stimulants: experience and exposure. This means that the sexually deviant child may have been molested or simply exposed to sexuality through pornography.[18]

In a study of six hundred American males and females of junior high school age and above, researcher Dr. Jennings Bryant found that 91 percent of the males and 82 percent of the females admitted having been exposed to X-rated, hard-core pornography. Over 66 percent of the males and 40 percent of the females reported wanting to try out some of the sexual behaviors they had witnessed. And among high schoolers, 31 percent of the males and 18 percent of the females admitted actually *doing* some of the things they had seen in the pornography within a few days after exposure.[19]

Exposure to Pornography Shapes Attitudes and Values

Most of us caring, responsible parents want to instill in our children our own personal values about relationships, sex, intimacy, love, and marriage. Unfortunately the powerful irresponsible messages of pornography may be educating our children on these very important life issues. Just as thirty-second commercials can influence whether or not we choose one popular soft drink over another, exposure to pornography shapes our attitudes and values and, often, our behavior.

Photographs, videos, magazines, virtual games, and Internet pornography that depict rape and the dehumanization of females in sexual scenes constitute powerful but deforming tools of sex education. The danger to children stems at least partly from the disturbing changes in attitude that are facilitated by pornography. Replicated studies [20] have demonstrated that exposure to significant amounts of increasingly graphic forms of pornography has a dramatic effect on how adult consumers view women, sexual abuse, sexual relationships, and sex in general. These studies are virtually unanimous in their conclusions: When male subjects were exposed to as little as six weeks' worth of standard hardcore pornography, they:

- developed an increased sexual callousness toward women
- began to trivialize rape as a criminal offense or no longer considered it a crime at all
- developed distorted perceptions about sexuality
- developed an appetite for more deviant, bizarre, or violent types of pornography (normal sex no longer seemed to do the job)
- devalued the importance of monogamy and lacked confidence in marriage as either a viable or lasting institution

- viewed nonmonogamous relationships as normal and natural behavior[21]

Much hard-core pornography promotes the "rape myth," teaching children that women enjoy having sex forced on them. Even soft-core pornography portrays women as objects who exist only to give sexual satisfaction to men. Furthermore, pornography teaches that sex is purely recreational. There is no emotional intimacy in pornography—only immediate physical satisfaction.[22]

The Centerfold Syndrome

Psychologist Dr. Gary R. Brooks, in his book, *The Centerfold Syndrome: How Men Can Overcome Objectification and Achieve Intimacy with Women,*[23] has identified four symptoms of the "centerfold syndrome." As the result of a steady diet of soft-core pornography, men may display one or more of the following symptoms:

- *Voyeurism*—an obsession with visual stimulation that trivializes all other features of a healthy relationship
- *Objectification*—obsessive fetishes over body parts and the rating of women by size and shape
- *Trophyism*—treatment of women as collectibles and property
- *Fear of intimacy*—inability to get beyond glossy, centerfold images of women to have a real relationship

Pornography subtly communicates that the value of a woman is determined by her body, shape, and size. Only those women with a perfect physical appearance are valuable and worthy of being admired, desired, and loved. This can have detrimental effects on how women and girls view themselves. I often wonder how many young girls who struggle with anorexia, bulimia, and other eating disorders are unknowingly struggling to measure up to the perfect "10" image projected by the airbrushed centerfold. I also wonder how many teenage boys, consciously or unconsciously, measure the value of their girlfriends against the "bunny" image.

Dr. Jennings Bryant comments:

> If the values which permeate the content of most hard-core pornography are examined, what is found is an almost total suspension of the sorts of moral judgment that have been espoused in the value systems of most civilized culture. Forget trust. Forget family. Forget commitment. Forget love. Forget marriage. Here, in this world of ultimate physical hedonism, anything goes. If we take seriously the social science research literature in areas such as social learning or cultivation effects, we should expect that the heavy consumer of hard-core pornography should acquire some of these values which are so markedly different from those of our mainstream society, especially if the consumer does not have a well developed value system of his or her own.[24]

Exposure to Pornography Interferes with a Child's Development and Identity

During certain critical periods of childhood, a child's brain is being programmed for sexual orientation. During this period, the mind appears to be developing a "hardwire" for what the person will be aroused by or attracted to. Exposure to healthy sexual norms and attitudes during this critical period can result in the child developing a healthy sexual orientation. In contrast, if there is exposure to pornography during this period, sexual deviance may become imprinted on the child's "hard drive" and become a permanent part of his or her sexual orientation.[25]

One psychologist's findings suggest that memories of experiences that occurred at times of emotional arousal (which could include sexual arousal) are imprinted on the brain by epinephrine, an adrenal gland hormone, and are difficult to erase.[26] (This may partly explain pornography's addicting effect.) Viewing pornography can potentially condition some viewers to have recurring sexual fantasies during which they masturbate. Later they may be tempted to act out the fantasies as sexual advances.

Sexual identity develops gradually through childhood and adolescence. In fact children generally do not have a *natural* sexual capacity until between the ages of ten and twelve. As they grow up, children are especially susceptible to influences affecting their development. Information about sex in most homes and schools, comes, presumably, in age-appropriate incremental stages based on what parents, educators, physicians, and social scientists have learned about child development. But pornography short-circuits and/or distorts the normal personality development process and supplies misinformation about a child's sexuality, sense of self, and body that leaves the child confused, changed, and damaged.[27]

Pornography often introduces children prematurely to sexual sensations that they are developmentally unprepared to contend with. This awareness of sexual sensation can be confusing and overstimulating. Feeling sexually aroused and sensing that one's body is damaged are not easy feelings for children to put into words. Sometimes they express these feelings through sexualized behaviors.[28]

The sexual excitement and eventual release obtained through pornography are mood altering. For example, if a young boy's early stimulus was pornographic photographs, he can be conditioned to become aroused through photographs. Once this pairing is rewarded a number of times, it is likely to become permanent.[29] The result is that it becomes difficult for the individual to experience sexual satisfaction apart from pornographic images.

Pornography also interferes with the emotional and spiritual development of children. The emotional harm may involve guilt, anger, depression, anxiety, phobias, panic disorders, and preoccupation with sexual behavior. There is a spiritual dimension to pornography addiction as well. Pornography gives the illusion that it will fill a spiritual void, but instead, it leaves its user spiritually empty.[30] Children who have been abused by or exposed to pornography often have difficulty trusting a God who allows them to experience feelings of shame, helplessness, and abandonment.

Pornography's Progressive Pattern

Dr. Victor Cline, a clinical psychologist at the University of Utah and a specialist in the area of sexual addictions, has observed a four-step syndrome common to almost all of his clients who have been involved with pornography.[31]

Step 1—Addiction. Once consumers of pornography get hooked, they keep coming back for more and more. The sexually graphic material provides the viewer with an aphrodisiac effect, followed by sexual release, most often through masturbation. Pornography gives the viewer powerful imagery that can be recalled and elaborated on with the person's fantasy life. Despite negative consequences, most addicts are unable to rid themselves of their dependence on pornography. Their addiction rules their lives.

Step 2—Escalation. Cline describes the second phase as an escalation-effect. The pornography consumer, similar to the drug user, requires more and more stimulation to reach his or her "highs." In fact some viewers prefer the powerful sexual imagery planted in their minds by exposure to pornography to sexual intercourse itself. This nearly always diminishes the viewer's capacity to love and express appropriate intimacy within relationships.

Step 3—Desensitization. In this phase, material that was originally perceived as unthinkable, shocking, illegal, repulsive, or immoral is now viewed as acceptable and commonplace by the viewer of pornography. Regardless of the deviancy expressed, the viewer perceives the pornography and his or her use of it as legitimate.

Step 4—Acting out sexually. This last step describes an increased tendency to act out sexually the behaviors viewed in pornography, including promiscuity, voyeurism, exhibitionism, group sex, rape, sadomasochism, child molestation, and more.

Clearly, this progressive pattern demonstrates how reality and fantasy become blurred for those who are entangled with pornography or when viewing is no longer enough.

In regard to the compulsive or addictive nature of pornography, Dr. Cline shares the following: "In over 26 years, I have treated approximately 350 males afflicted with sexual addictions (or sometimes referred to as sexual compulsions). In about 94 percent of the cases I have found that pornography was a contributor, facilitator, or direct causal agent in the acquiring of these sexual illnesses."[32]

One of Dr. Cline's patients was so deeply addicted that he could not stay away from pornography for ninety days, even for one thousand dollars. While the client was extremely committed to quitting to save his marriage, live in harmony with his religious principles, and regain his money, he succumbed to his appetite for pornography.[33]

The Symptoms of Sexual Disturbance among Children

Parents, teachers, and guardians may find it difficult to distinguish between normal and healthy childhood sexual experimentation and sexual deviance resulting from exposure to pornography. The following guidelines, established by mental health and law enforcement officials, are useful in assessing sexual disturbance among children.[34]

These guidelines can also help to identify the symptoms of psychological damage resulting from exposure to sexual material on the Internet.

Sexual Preoccupation

Children who have been harmed by viewing pornography may be excessively curious about or overly preoccupied with sexuality. Some children expose their genitals to others or engage in a sudden, unusually high level of masturbation.

Age-Inappropriate Sexualized Behavior

Some children may display sexual knowledge and behavior beyond that which is appropriate for their age. This is one of the few reliable and distinguishing characteristics that identify sexually abused children.[35] Very young children may enact adult sexual scenarios and behaviors in their play with other children or with their dolls and stuffed animals.

Age-Inappropriate Partners

Having learned the message that sexual overtures are acceptable ways to get attention and rewards, children may enter into unhealthy relationships, particularly with older, age-inappropriate partners. Additionally, believing the myth generated by pornography that their bodies are for the use of others, young girls may become promiscuous. Children preoccupied with sex may attempt to engage younger children in sexual behavior because younger and smaller children are easier to manipulate and often more cooperative.

Coercion

Aggressive attempts to undress, sexually touch, or attempt intercourse with others are not uncommon among sexually preoccupied children. When a tendency toward secretive play combines with intense sexual preoccupation, a child may be vulnerable to repeating his or her abuse with other children in ways that can create chaos and further victimization. A child who is internally driven to do to others what has been done to him or her requires extensive parental supervision and therapeutic help.[36]

Paraphilias

One of the most harmful effects that sexually deviant pornography can have on children is the later development of paraphilias—that is, any group of persistent sexual behavior patterns in which unusual objects, rituals, or situations are required for full sexual satisfaction. Fetishes, voyeurism, exhibitionism, sexual sadism, sexual masochism, eroticized urination and defecation, bestiality, and pedophilia all fit into this category. In addition to the possibility of permanently altering a child's sexual orientation toward the development of paraphilias, sexually deviant pornography may contribute to the development of deviant sexual morals, attitudes, and beliefs.

Helping Children Deal with Trauma Inflicted by Pornography

The best way to reduce the suffering of a child traumatized by pornography on the Internet (or by any other medium) is to prevent pornography from entering the child's life. In chapters 5, 6, and 7, we will look at some prevention tactics and technological solutions. While we all strive to protect our children from trauma, we are not always successful. If *your* child tells you that he or she has seen or read something on the Internet of a sexual nature or has had contact with a sexual predator and appears to be experiencing some trauma from that experience, talk with your child about it and, if necessary, seek professional help. Identifying, and sometimes discussing, the signs and symptoms of psychological damage is a first step to relieving the child's suffering. Try to provide opportunities to talk about feelings. When hearing and accepting a child's feelings are too difficult, therapy involving the child and the family is often necessary.

Helping a child deal with trauma involves adjusting expectations regarding the child's behavior and coping ability. Because the force of a psychological trauma disrupts the development of the child, it is normal to expect a traumatized child to regress. When children regress, parents need to match their responses to the needs of a younger child. Some children show increased fearfulness following a trauma. A helpful approach for a parent in this situation might be to acknowledge the fear and offer help and support. Older children can be reminded of fears they overcame in the past.

The following is a recommended strategy if you think your child has been abused, traumatized, or sexually exploited while on the Internet:

- Believe your child! Children rarely lie about sexual abuse or trauma.
- Commend your child for telling you about his or her experience.
- Convey your support for your child. Your child may fear that he or she is at fault and responsible for viewing the pornography or interacting with a sexual predator. Try to alleviate this self-blame.
- Temper your own reaction. Recognize that your response sends a critical message to your child. Your greatest challenge may be to not convey your own horror.
- Report the suspected illegal online activity to your local police. In some communities the local police department is equipped to investigate computer crimes, such as online solicitation of a minor. Also report such incidences to the CyberTipline: 800-843-5678 (www.missingkids.com/cybertip).
- Locate a specialized agency that evaluates sexual abuse or trauma victims—a hospital, a community mental health therapy group, or a child advocate agency.
- If your child has been physically abused as a result of contact with an online predator, contact a physician with experience and training in detecting sexual abuse.

- Talk with your child's teachers, baby-sitters, other parents, and adults who have supervised your child online.[37]

This is a dark chapter because pornography in cyberspace casts a dangerous shadow on our children. Most of us find it difficult to talk to our children about sex in general, let alone the harmful effects of pornography, as graphically described in this chapter. We want to protect the innocence and purity of childhood for as long as possible. Yet children need to know why certain rules about the computer and their access to the Internet exist. They may be less likely to violate the rules if they are told the truth about why they are not allowed to see everything on the Internet. In the next chapter we will look at how we can begin to educate our children about protecting themselves from dangers in cyberspace.

Cybersavvy Quiz #3

Take the following quiz on pornography. Then reread this chapter to get more specific information on areas that are confusing or unclear.

1. Child pornography:
   a. reduces dangerous impulses
   b. is harmless entertainment
   c. is not protected by the First Amendment
2. Pornography promotes:
   a. healthier relationships between men and women
   b. positive images of women
   c. unsafe sex

3. Symptoms of sexual disturbance among children are:
   a. the same for every child
   b. unnoticeable
   c. age-inappropriate sexualized behaviors
4. The best strategy for helping a child who has been traumatized is:
   a. don't tell anyone about the incident
   b. check out the child's story because children are prone to lie
   c. try to alleviate any self-blame for viewing pornography or interacting with a sexual predator
5. A steady diet of soft-core pornography may result in the following:
   a. a better relationship with one's spouse
   b. more respect for women in general
   c. voyeurism

Scoring: If you chose answer C for every question, you answered correctly. Congratulations! If you missed several answers, take some time to reread this chapter.

For further information on pornography, refer to the following resources and see appendix D.

Protecting Children in Cyberspace, Stephen J. Kavanagh
Centerfold Syndrome: How Men Can Overcome Objectification and Achieve Intimacy with Women, Gary Brooks

*How can I build a trust
relationship with my child?*

*When are children ready to use
a computer or go online?*

*What should I tell my child about the risks
and dangers of cyberspace?*

*What kinds of rules and limitations
regarding online activity do I need
to set for my child?*

5
The First Line of Defense

Susan sat on Lily's bed and thought about the pornographic e-mail her daughter had received.

Thank goodness, I was here when it happened! And thank goodness, Lily talked to me about it! But what if I hadn't been home? What if she had replied to the message or seen something even worse on the screen?

The encounter had confirmed Susan's greatest fears about having a computer with Internet access—a dangerous stranger from cyberspace had approached her daughter there in her own family room . . . and in Susan's presence!

Susan didn't want to restrict Lily's online time. That would be punishing Lily for the stranger's intrusion. At the same time, she was more determined than ever to make sure that Lily's online experience would be safe.

"Mom, I'm sorry about reading the e-mail and seeing that picture," Lily said softly, hanging her head as she sat down next to Susan.

"It's not your fault, Lily," Susan responded as she put her arm around Lily's waist and pulled her closer. "In fact it's really your dad's and my responsibility to take some safety precautions. And we should have sat down as a family and set some safety rules for all of us when we go online."

"What if the person who sent that stuff to me comes to our house?"

"I don't think there's any way for that person to know where we live, Lily," Susan said calmly. "But even if the person discovers where we live, your dad and I can protect you, along with the police and Murphy."

"Murphy's just a little dog!"

"Ahhh, he may be a little dog but he has a very big bark that lets Daddy and me know if anyone is in our yard or near the house. We can count on him!"

Most parents wouldn't dream of sending a nine year old into a new situation—the first day at a new school, the first time at a new playground, the first time without supervision at a large mall—without explaining what to expect and defining acceptable behavior for that new situation. But like Susan, many parents do not realize the same principle applies to the Internet. Parents need to establish the rules for the Information Superhighway, spelling out what kids can do, what they should avoid, and how to respond to messages and material that make them uncomfortable.

The TV set served as a baby-sitter for many years until the arrival of the personal home computer. Many of us couch potatoes sat for hours watching *The Andy Griffith Show*, *The Brady Bunch*, and our favorite cartoons. Whereas TV may have sequestered us into a world of our own, computer use—particularly, Internet use—puts us in contact with a large number of people throughout the world. For this reason, when children use the Internet, specific guidelines need to be in place. The ideal is that an adult is present and involved. When a latchkey child, who arrives home several hours before a parent, or a lonely child with low esteem has unrestricted access to the Internet, he or she is vulnerable and at risk.

Just as parental involvement is necessary to help children avoid other pitfalls in life, such as alcohol or drug abuse, our active participation in online experiences is critical. We bear the primary responsibility for teaching our children to be wise and safe on the Internet. To do that, we need to be aware of practical and helpful resources, safety tips, and technological solutions that guard against online risks. In an era of two-career families and single-parent families, however, many of us cannot do the job alone. It may not be possible (or even desirable) for parents to supervise their children all of the time, and the home is not the only point of access to the Internet. The problem is further complicated by the fact that some parents are not yet computer literate.

Ultimately we must educate our children about online safety, including the possibility of encountering pornographic material and pedophiles. Depending on their age, this may mean exploring cyberspace alongside our children, implementing software solutions (we'll talk about those in chapter 6), and talking to them about the real dangers of the Internet. We must ensure our children's protection online and be mentors for wise decision making.

Establishing an Atmosphere of Trust

Regardless of your level of technical know-how now, it is important for you to become comfortable using your computer and the Internet. Then you will be able to discuss intelligently with your child online experiences that either of you have. Maintaining a continuing dialogue with your child is one of the keys to building an atmosphere of trust around your computer. If you want to encourage such an atmosphere, then you must make it clear to your child that he or she can safely bring online incidents to your attention without being blamed or having the Internet banned from your home. If you neglect to build a trust relationship with your child, you will probably never hear what happens online, whether in your home, at school, or in the library.

In a recent *20/20* interview a group of teenagers were asked if they had ever encountered pornography or sexual predators online. The answer was a unanimous "yes." When asked if they shared this disturbing information with their parents, the answer was an overwhelming "no way!"

Trust building must be an intentional process. It doesn't happen automatically. It requires commitment and time, and your children may test you on both of these. There is no substitute for spending quality time with a child over an extended period. By regularly committing to going online together (for example, ten to twenty minutes a day), you can experience educational and recreational adventures that bring you and your child closer together.

You can build a trust relationship with your child by giving him or her a problem-solving task that requires your child to work side by side with you or another family member. For example, you might ask your computer-literate child to help you locate some information online about how to build a birdhouse. As the two of you search the Internet, discover and discuss solutions, and help each other accomplish the goal, bonds will be built. Cooperation is your main goal. As you accept and welcome your child's input, he or she will begin to recognize the value of his or her opinion and computer literacy.

When children perceive that we are genuinely interested in them, they will be more willing to trust us with their insecurities, frustrations, and fears. Sadly the opposite is also true. If they perceive that we don't care to listen, trust will not be built. Take opportunities to talk with and listen to your child around the dinner table or on the way to school. Parents need to stimulate discussion, dialogue, and a sharing of ideas. Every time you get together, ask questions of each other, exchange views, weigh decisions together, air feelings. This disclosure will draw you closer together. Try to get beyond the small talk and share deeply with your child. This does not mean you must bare your soul, but rather that you are honest and open with him or her. The more empathic you are, the more secure your child will feel when sharing with you a distressing or uncomfortable experience on the Internet.

In a healthy family each person feels included and appreciated. If a child is shy or less outgoing than other children, make sure he or she is affirmed and accepted. Affirming your child's value and unique abilities is crucial to the growing process of trust. This affirmation can come in relationship to the computer. Compliment your child for his or her grasp of the technology or for a discovery he or she has made online. Your affirmation encourages your child to share deeper experiences and feelings. Many reclusive children become more active and self-confident as they become more aware of their family's admiration and respect for them and their technological giftedness. Try telling your child why you appreciate him or her and what strengths you admire, particularly in the area of computer skills and savvy. Kids need positive feedback to reassure them that others think they are okay. Then they feel free to be open about their feelings and experiences.

When children are able to express their anger, struggles, and frustrations with what they may perceive as our overprotectiveness regarding Web surfing, we need to respond with empathy, support, and encouragement. Then we will be able to talk through possible solutions to the potential dangers that concern us regarding the Internet and set guidelines for appropriate behavior and safe conduct online. Our calm, grounded approach will give us a foundation from which to hold our children accountable while giving them some freedom to fail.

 CAUTION

Computer Safety

It is *very* important that you place your computer in a central family location. This will enable you to supervise the computer without always actively participating with your child.

Rules for the Road

Children hear about the wonders and exciting places to visit on the Internet from their friends, their teachers, and the media. Unfortunately they don't hear often enough about the risks of Internet use—except from their parents. We must accept the preventive (and often criticized) role of setting limits that keep our kids safe from harmful material and predators. There are ten concerns that I believe every parent should discuss with his or her child as soon as the child begins to use the Internet, regardless of his or her age.

Top 10 Things to Tell Your Child

1. *Never* fill out questionnaires or any forms online or give out personal information (such as name, age, address, phone number, school, town, password, schedule) about yourself or anyone else to anyone without Mom and/or Dad's permission.
2. *Never* agree to meet in person with anyone you have spoken to online without Mom and/or Dad's presence.
3. *Never* enter a chat room without Mom and/or Dad's presence or supervision. Some "kids" you meet in chat rooms may not really be kids; they may be adults with bad intentions. Remember, people may not be who they say they are.
4. *Never* tell anyone online where you will be or what you will be doing without Mom and/or Dad's permission.
5. *Never* respond to or send e-mail to new people you meet online.
6. *Never* go into a new online area that is going to cost additional money without first getting Mom and/or Dad's permission.
7. *Never* send, without Mom and/or Dad's permission, a picture over the Internet or via regular mail to anyone you've met on the Internet.
8. *Never* buy or order products online or give out any credit card information online without Mom and/or Dad's permission.
9. *Never* respond to any belligerent or suggestive contact or anything that makes you feel uncomfortable. End such an experience by *logging off* and telling Mom and/or Dad as soon as possible.
10. *Always* tell Mom and/or Dad about something you saw, intentionally or unintentionally, that is upsetting. (It is better for your child's mental health

to be able to discuss exposure to pornography than for it to become a dark and confusing secret.[1])

When Is My Child Ready to Go Online?

While going online together is a wonderful opportunity to instill cautious and responsible use of the Internet into your child, I realize that this may not be a realistic option for many parents. So let me just suggest that whenever possible, join your child as he or she explores the valuable resources on online. If your child knows more about getting around the Internet than you do, ask him or her to be *your* guide! This is a great way for you to empower and build self-confidence in your child. Sharing the experience of surfing the Net is an effective, proactive parenting technique. Leaving kids alone for hours at a time on the Internet is not. Check the computer screen periodically and let your children know that you are interested in what they are learning online. Just as watching a TV program with your child is more effective than letting him or her watch alone, surfing the Net together gives you the opportunity to answer questions and talk about anything that comes up.

Determining when a child is ready to go online does not depend on a child's capability to use a computer. In her book, *A Parent's Guide to the Internet*, Parry Aftab shares how her niece was able to *boot* up a computer, load a *CD-ROM*, and play a game when she was only three years old.[2] Of course, this child had been introduced to a computer when she was ten months old, sitting on her parent's lap. Between her first and third birthdays, her parents guided her hand on the mouse, let her play with an old keyboard, and allowed her to play games designed for toddlers.

Not all parents have the time or desire to take this kind of initiative with their young children. However, we may have to reconsider how early to begin preparing our children as the Digital Age encroaches on their lives. Who knows? Perhaps in the future some level of computer literacy may be required for graduation from preschool or kindergarten!

Very little formal research has been done to identify how information technology affects children of different ages and when is the best time to start various activities, such as computer usage. But common sense tells us that younger children need more supervision than older ones. In chapter 6 we'll talk about software for your computer that can restrict access. Younger children, of course, would need more restrictive software tools to safeguard their online experiences. As kids get older, less supervision and less restrictive software measures may be required. In addition, children differ in their maturity, emotional development, and skills. The Children's Partnership, a national nonprofit organization with a mission to raise public awareness about the needs of America's children, has developed some age-appropriate guidelines, based on the advice of child development experts. The following tips, adapted from their *Parents' Guide to the Information Superhighway*, are given for the earliest age group applicable. They may, however, apply at later stages as well.[3]

Ages Two to Three

Computers need not play much of a role in a two- to three-year-old's life, but you may choose to introduce your toddler to computers. A child's motor skills become more highly developed between eighteen and twenty-four months. At that age you may want to let your child sit in your lap and tap the keyboard and touch the mouse. Put your hand over your child's on the mouse to show how it works. While a little one's tiny hands won't work well initially on adult-size accessories, you may be surprised at how adept your child will become if he or she has regular contact with a computer. There are games and interactive activities on CD-ROMs or other software (rather than online activities) that are geared to the level of a two to three year old.

> The Children's Partnership (http://www.childrenspartner ship.org) is a national, nonprofit organization with a mission to increase public awareness of children's needs and engage leaders and the public in finding ways to help children. It offers online, for free, the full text of its useful guide *The Parents' Guide to the Information Superhighway: Rules and Tools for Families Online* (1998), prepared by The Children's Partnership with the National PTA and the National Urban League. A printed version of the guide is also available.

Ages Four to Seven

Children at this age begin to make greater use of computer games and educational products. Older children in this age range, with their parents, may also begin exploring online children's areas. Children learn intuitively and quickly, but at this age they still depend on parents for reading and interpreting directions.

Between the ages of four and seven, children begin to form their first friendships, grasp the basics of gender differences, and acquire morally relevant rules and behaviors. This is a good time to begin talking about rules for using the computer and going online.

Spend as much time as you can with your child while he or she uses the computer. Print work your child has done on the computer or resources he or she has found

Disney's CyberNetiquette Comix series is a public education program developed to give families a fun and interactive way to learn valuable lessons about online safety. Launched as part of Daily Blast's first annual "AwareNet Week," the first episode features the Three Little Pigs in "Who's Afraid of Little Sweet Sheep?" and covers the basic rule of never giving one's address or personal information out to anyone on the Internet. It uses the classic Three Little Pigs characters to show that people aren't always who they seem to be, online or off. The content of the CyberNetiquette Comix series was designed to encourage parents and children to enjoy it together and then discuss the online awareness tips presented in each series. CyberNetiquette Comix can be accessed from Disney.com and AwareNet.com.

on the Internet. You and your child should have the same address, so you can oversee his or her mail and discuss correspondence. Check with your child's teachers and librarians for suggestions for good online activities.

Ages Eight to Eleven

At eight to eleven years of age most children begin to directly encounter and appreciate more fully the potential of online experiences. For example, they can begin to use online encyclopedias to do research and

My Rules for Online Safety

I never give out or send personal information (photos, addresses, telephone numbers, or location of school) without my parent's permission.

If I come across or I am sent information online that makes me feel uncomfortable, I'll tell my parents or teacher and I will not respond to this kind of message.

I'll never agree to get together with someone I meet online without my parent's prior knowledge and consent.

TEACHERS: Sexually explicit images, sent to or depicting a child, are against the law. Report violations to the National Center for Missing and Exploited Children's (NCMEC) toll-free tipline, 1-800-843-5678. This educational campaign is conducted in cooperation with the U.S. Customs Service, the U.S. Postal Inspection Service, and the Federal Bureau of Investigation.

"My Rules for Online Safety" is taken from the mousepad of the National Center for Missing and Exploited Children. The mouse pad is being distributed to elementary and middle schools as they are connected to the Internet. Some of the pads have been paid for with federal funds, but most have been financed with private funds from the computer industry. These tips are adapted from Child Safety on the Information Highway by Lawrence J. Magid. They are reprinted with permission of the National Center for Missing and Exploited Children (NCMEC). Copyright NCMEC 1994. All rights reserved.

download graphics and photos for school reports. They may correspond via e-mail with pen pals around the world. They may also be exchanging information with faraway relatives and online friends. Be aware of your child's e-mail habits and do not allow correspondence with strangers. Get to know your children's online friends just as you would get to know their friends at school or in the neighborhood. Remember, even in cyberspace, the most vulnerable children are those with low self-esteem. Encourage your children to find friends and interests outside of the Internet.

Just as many conscientious parents limit the amount of time that their children spend watching movies and TV or playing video games, they need to apply the same principle to online time. Set clear guidelines as to how much time is spent online. Even if a child's online experience is educational, recreational, and enriching, relating to a machine will never offer the benefits of relating to other people face-to-face. If you observe your child withdrawing from family or friends to sit at the computer, you may want to reduce the amount of time your child is spending both on the computer and on the Internet. Help your child to learn not to rely on a computer for companionship.

Children between the ages of nine and eleven are the most likely victims of child sexual abuse.[4] Make sure that your child is aware that not all "friends" whom he or she meets on the Internet will be well meaning. Teach your child to end any experience online when he or she feels uncomfortable or scared by logging off and telling you or a trusted adult as soon as possible. Discuss the unique aspect of anonymous behavior in cyberspace and what it means for your child and others. Explain to your child that many of the people that he or she will meet on the Internet do not use their real identities. For example, a man may identify himself as a woman, or, in some cases, adults may attempt to pass themselves off as children. Explain that while these actions may seem funny and harmless, many children are often seduced and lured into dangerous situations by such predators.

As your child moves toward independence, you need to stay "hands-on" and help guide him or her to appropriate online content. Children of this age are also prime targets for programmers and advertisers. Help your child evaluate content and understand what's behind advertising. Marketers have devised a variety of techniques to compile personal information and profiles on children. Tracking technologies make it possible to monitor every interaction between a child and an advertisement.[5] Discuss the difference between advertising and educational or entertainment content. Show your child examples of each. Begin to show your child the difference between sources of information that are credible and those that are not.

Netiquette

Parents are ultimately responsible for teaching their children to be good "netizens" and to follow "netiquette." Since children may meet people from all over the world on the Internet, teach your child to respect other people and their ideas. Occasionally people do and say things online that they would never ordinarily do or say face-to-face. Caution your child that on the Internet, everything said is traceable and nothing said is truly anonymous. Encourage your child to avoid flames (strong messages that may include obscenities to provoke anger or an argument) and to not use rude or bad language online. Many providers will terminate your account if you do.

E-Mail Abbreviations

BTW	by the way
CC	carbon copy
CUL8R	see you later
FAQ	frequently asked question
FWIW	for what it's worth
FYI	for your information

IMHO	in my humble opinion
IMO	in my opinion
IOW	in other words
LOL	laughing out loud
OTOH	on the other hand
PMJI	pardon me for jumping in
RE	regarding
ROFL	rolling on the floor laughing
TIA	thanks in advance
TTFN	tata for now
WRT	with respect to
YMMV	your mileage may vary (you may get different results)

Emoticons

Icon	Keystrokes	What It Means
:-)	colon, hyphen, right parenthesis	smile
;-)	semi-colon, hyphen, right parenthesis	wink
:-(	colon, hyphen, left parenthesis	frown
:-D	colon, hyphen, capital D	laughing
:'-O	colon, apostrophe, hyphen, capital O	crying
:-o	colon, hyphen, lowercase o	surprised
:-O	colon, hyphen, capital O	very surprised
:-*	colon, hyphen, asterisk	a kiss for you
:-P	colon, hyphen, capital P	sticking out your tongue

If you need to emphasize a word, use asterisks, like *this.*

Ages Twelve to Fourteen

Adolescents are capable of using the sophisticated research resources of the Internet, accessing everything from the Library of Congress's collection of magazines and newspapers to letters and archives from around the world.

Just as most teenagers are interested in chatting on the phone, many will want to be involved in chatting online. Some online commercial services have chat rooms that are appropriate for preteens and teenagers. However, as I have mentioned previously, these areas are often the playgrounds of pedophiles, criminals, and unscrupulous marketers who may target your child.

According to Ernie Allen, president of the National Center for Missing and Exploited Children, thirteen- to fifteen-year-old teenagers are at the greatest risk of sexual exploitation by Internet predators. NCMEC has produced a brochure, "Teen Safety on the Information Highway," which is an excellent resource for you and your teenager. (See appendix A for the address, phone number, and e-mail address of NCMEC.)

While you (and your teen!) may feel that he or she doesn't need the same restrictions that are placed on younger children, I want to encourage you to consider the risks of allowing your teenager unlimited Internet freedom. This age group is more likely to explore out-of-the-way nooks and crannies in cyberspace. They're also more likely to reach out to people outside their peer groups. And because they're more likely to explore on their own, they are more easily preyed upon by pedophiles and other sexual predators.[6]

Parents must set up clear rules for teenagers. This means agreements about Internet access at and away from home, time limits, and periodic check-ins. Help your child understand the laws governing online behavior (including pornography, predators, and stalking) and the consequences to them or anyone else for breaking them. Remind your son or daughter that possession, distribution, and production of some pornographic material is illegal. Ask your teenager very specific questions like:

- Have you seen any pornographic pictures?
- Has anyone online talked dirty to you?
- Have you met anyone online whom you don't know?
- Has anyone asked you for personal information?
- Has anyone asked to meet you in person?

If you decide to allow your teen to spend some time in chat rooms, clarify the rules and decide which groups are acceptable. Because chat rooms can be so dangerous, I recommend that you supervise your child whenever he or she enters that area. The exception would be monitored chat rooms offered by some online services. Discuss with your young teen what actions he or she can take if people harass or do anything inappropriate online.

If your teen has computer magazines, review them and discuss any objectionable material. Don't forget to look at ads, new games, and software packages. If you find questionable products in your child's possession, take the time to have a discussion about them. Pay attention to games that your teen has downloaded or copied. Many are great fun, but others are extremely violent. A good way to dissolve the atmosphere of trust that you have attempted to create with your child is by destroying one of his or her games or CD-ROMs. Remember: Trust works both ways. Discuss why a game or program is objectionable and allow your teen to decide that it's not worth having in his or her library.

CAUTION

Parents often ask, "What are the signs that my child has a problem with pornography on the Internet?" Here are a few warnings:

- Your child is hiding disks.
- Your child spends an inordinate amount of time on the Internet or is online late into the night.
- Your child uses computer files that end in .gif or .jpg. These are picture files that may contain the latest Hubble telescope photos, a picture of Grandma's parakeet, or pornographic material.
- You discover unusual charges on your credit card statements. Be especially suspicious of phone charges that identify themselves as "Web Site." Many pornographers don't provide their names to avoid raising parental concern.
- Your child quickly changes the computer screen when you enter the room.[7]

Ages Fifteen to Nineteen

Teenagers often want to have a computer in their bedroom. In spite of a teenager's need for privacy and independence, I do not recommend that a computer with Internet access be placed in his or her bedroom. It's very difficult for a parent to monitor a teen's online activities when the computer is behind a closed door. Some parents have reported seeing a blue glow coming from under their teen's door in the middle of the night. Later when they received their phone bill, they put the puzzle together and discovered unauthorized computer use.

When it comes to Internet access, keeping the computer in a common area of the home is the safest option.

Older teens can use the Internet to search for information about job opportunities, internships, and colleges or universities. With their increased skills, curiosity, and freedom come more ways to run into undesirable and even dangerous experiences. Parents must find creative ways to stay in touch with their teenage children about online activities.

For Parents Only

- Become more computer literate and develop Internet savvy so that you can keep up-to-date on products, news, and opinions surrounding the issues of children's safety on the Internet.
- Place your computer in an area of your home where you can easily monitor your child's Internet activity.
- Talk with your kids about their online friends and activities.
- Implement parental controls available on your online service, install protective software on your home computer, or use a clean ISP (see chapter 6).
- Block adult chat rooms and instant/personal messages from people you and your child don't know (see chapter 6).
- Some OSPs (Online Service Providers), such as America Online, offer subscribers online profiles. Do not permit your child to have an online profile. With this restriction, he or she will not be listed in directories and is less likely to be approached in chat rooms where pedophiles often search for prey.
- Many Internet sites allow children to set up free home pages. Discuss with your child what information he or she can have on the page. For example, interests and hobbies are probably okay, but a home phone number is not!

◀ • Check with your child's school to see if kids' projects, artwork, or photos (where material is identified by name) are
being put on school home pages. Schools often want to post
school newsletters or sports scores, but every time a full
name is displayed, there is vulnerability. Schools need to be
reminded of that risk.

• Monitor the amount of time your child spends on the Internet, and at what times of day. Excessive time online, especially at night, may indicate a problem.

• Establish online rules and an agreement with your child
about Internet use away from home (i.e., at a friend's house,
at school, at the library, etc.).

• Watch for changes in your child's behavior (mention of adults
you don't know, secretiveness, inappropriate sexual knowledge, sleeping problems, etc.).

House Rules

Every family should draft their own Internet use policy. In appendix E: Sample House Rules, you will find
several sample family contracts or Internet use policies
from which to draw ideas for your own house rules.

When you sit down with your family to write the rules
for *your* house, keep in mind the top ten list of concerns
given on page 107. Your rules should govern *every* family member's behavior online. House rules should help
your child understand proper netiquette, what to expect
from others online, how to respond when something
unexpected occurs, and how to protect oneself in cyberspace.[8]

The possible scenarios in the following family pledge
were adopted from *Get CyberSavvy!* and may help you
make choices regarding your own house rules.[9]

Being Cybersavvy: Your Family Pledge

I (we), member(s) of the _____ family, believe it is my (our) duty to use the Internet responsibly and safely and to follow the pledge we have created for our family. By signing this agreement, I (we) promise to explore the Internet safely and to uphold the responsibilities we have written below.

If I want to explore parts of the Internet or an online service, I will _____

If a person I meet online asks for my address, phone number, school name, password, or other personal information, I will _____

If I receive a scary or threatening e-mail message, I will _____

If I want to visit a Web site or play a game and have to fill out a registration form, I will _____

If I want to buy something from a store I have visited online, I will _____

If I come across pornography, I will _____

If someone says something to me online that makes me feel uncomfortable, I will _____

If someone I meet online asks to see me in person, I will _____

Special Family Amendments

If _____

I will _____

Signed, _____

On the _____ day of _____ in the year _____

Breaking the Rules

In the event that you discover your child has violated your house rules, try to meet the transgression with an appropriate discipline. For example, replying to unsolicited e-mail that contains obscenities is a far worse (and more dangerous) offense than spending too much time online.

If your child has received, downloaded, printed, viewed, or uploaded a pornographic message or photo, consider suspending his or her Internet privileges. Take the opportunity to discuss the dangers of viewing pornography and how viewing more and more pornography is harmful and may lead to sexual addiction. Share one of the stories from chapter 3 on how pornography can easily become a destructive habit. If you would like more information on how to provide for child safety online, check appendix A: Resources for Kids and Parents.

I'm often asked how I make my own family's experience online a safe one. At first, my husband, Jack, and I had Internet access at our offices and so we elected not to have an online service at home. Knowing what is available on the Internet with a few clicks of a mouse, we didn't feel we would be able to properly monitor our computer-literate teenagers as much as we'd like to since we both work full-time.

Recently we purchased a home computer and after careful evaluation, we have chosen a major service as our Internet provider. Jack and I have instituted our own house rules for behavior, both online and off.

To teach Sean and Mindy how to conduct themselves as responsible teenagers and, later, adults, my husband, Jack, often uses the following word picture to make it easier for them to visualize the concept. It goes something like this:

> *Jack's Box:* Picture your life as operating inside a box. As you consistently demonstrate increasing levels of personal responsibility, the box gets larger, and your world of opportunity increases. When you do not act responsibly, the box shrinks, and we start over again. As the parent responsible for training you in the right way to live, I control the box. At a point in the future, when you have reached adulthood, I expect to turn the control of your box over to you.

In regard to Internet use, as our children comply with general safety practices, our specific house rules, and their school's Internet policy, their freedoms may be expanded. With violations and demonstrations of broken trust, Internet and computer privileges are restricted.

In addition to house rules, we utilize the *parental controls* on our ISP. In the next chapter, we'll look at the technological solutions available to parents, including parental controls and blocking and filtering software programs.

Your supervision and communication of expectations are the keys to your child having a safe and enjoyable experience on the Internet. While the technological solutions in chapter 6 will provide some protection and safety features, no software will substitute for your supervision. Parry Aftab suggests that new young netizens should be issued a learner's permit to surf the Web, one that requires an adult's presence with the child until he or she can pass the test for a full-fledged license to surf.[10] Use the suggestions and age-appropriate guidelines in this chapter to help your child earn that license to drive on the Information Superhighway.

Cybersavvy Quiz #4

Take the following quiz to see how cybersavvy you are. Then review this chapter or use the glossary to get more specific information on areas that are confusing or unclear.

1. I can build an atmosphere of trust by:
   a. going online with my child
   b. asking my child to teach me about the Internet
   c. telling my child how much I admire his or her computer savvy
   d. all of the above
2. One of the factors for determining when a child should be allowed to go online is:
   a. the child's age
   b. how well the child understands the safety rules for going online
   c. the child's maturity, emotional development, and skills
   d. all of the above
3. Emoticons are:
   a. how people online express emotions
   b. made up of letters and symbols
   c. usually looked at sideways
   d. all of the above
4. You should tell your child to never:
   a. offer personal information to someone online without your permission
   b. buy or order a product online with your credit card without your permission
   c. go to chat rooms without your permission
   d. all of the above
5. A good time to set and enforce online guidelines is:
   a. when your child is 4–7 years old

b. when your child is 8–11 years old
c. when your child is 12–14 years old
d. all of the above

Scoring: If you chose answer D for every question, you answered correctly. Congratulations! If you missed several answers, take some time to reread this chapter and become more familiar with these terms as you work through this book and go online more often.

For further information on protecting children in cyberspace, refer to the following resources and see appendix A.

The Parents' Guide to the Information Superhighway: Rules and Tools for Families Online, The Children's Partnership

Teen Safety on the Information Highway, National Center for Missing and Exploited Children

*Is it really necessary to use protective
software or parental controls if
I trust my child?*

*What's the difference between end-user soft-
ware and server-based software controls?*

*Which commercial online services
offer parental controls?*

*What types of technological tools
should I implement?*

6
Creating a Digital Toolbox

Susan and Tom sat together in the family room
looking through all the information on filters,
blockers, browsers, monitors, closed systems, and
ratings systems for the Internet.

"How are we supposed to know which of these
things to use?" Susan asked. "After that incident
with Lily's e-mail, I think we need more than just
house rules for Internet access. Isn't there more
that we can do to protect her when she's online?"

"We're just going to have to take the time to dig
through all of this material until we understand
it," Tom replied. "And until we come up with some
better options, we had better make sure we are
around whenever Lily's on the Internet. I don't
know if we can trust the parental controls on our
ISP."

"I think we need to get something that will limit her to just the good Web sites that are appropriate for children," commented Susan, "but I was talking to Jane yesterday afternoon, and she said that those closed systems that contain only good sites are too restrictive. She says that while they block out pornography, they also end up preventing kids from going to sites where additional good content can be found. I just don't know what to believe."

"That's why we need to do some exploring ourselves," Tom suggested. "Maybe we can find a solution that gives us protection with an option for us to override the blocking for our own use."

When it comes to the Internet, parents worry about pornography and sexual predators. But when it comes to precautions, surprisingly few moms and dads are taking advantage of the commercially available filtering and blocking software that helps to protect children from the unsavory side of life in cyberspace.[1]

In 1997 President Clinton announced an expansive plan to build a family-friendly Internet:

> The computer industry is developing a whole toolbox full of technologies. . . . They give parents the power to unlock—or to lock the digital doors to objectionable content. Now we have to make these tools more readily available to all parents and all teachers in America, and as new tools come on line, we have to distribute them quickly and we have to make sure that parents are trained to use them. I think it's fair to say that all parents will likely lag behind their children in facility on the Internet, but at least if we understand the tools that are available, it will be possible to do the responsible and correct thing. With a combination of technology, law enforcement and parental responsibilities, we have the best chance to ensure that the Internet will be both safe for our children and the greatest educational resource we have ever known.[2]

The White House plan called for cooperation from the Internet industry to provide parents (and teachers) with "easy-to-use" child protection technology. As Tom and Susan have discovered, child protection technology is abundant, but information on determining which technology is appropriate for your home and how to implement each tool is less plentiful and a bit more difficult to understand.

> President Clinton's message is consistent with a three-pronged approach promoted and facilitated at Enough Is Enough for making the Internet safe for children. It involves the public, the technology industry, and law enforcement sharing the responsibility for implementing safe solutions.

At the Internet Online Summit: Focus on Children in late 1997, leaders from the following sectors—industry, education/parent/family, consumer advocacy, child advocacy, and law enforcement—joined together to respond to President Clinton's challenge. The technological objectives that resulted from the Summit were:

- to encourage the continued development and deployment of user empowerment tools that will assist parents and others responsible for children in shielding those children from material they deem inappropriate and shaping children's communication and information options online;
- to enable access to positive, appropriate content and communications based on individual values;
- to enable service and content providers and others to create family-friendly environments.

Unlike the TV V-chip, a great variety of Internet parental empowerment tools are available today and capable of serving online families with diverse values, without infringing on the First Amendment rights of Internet users. Parents with home Internet access have the option to filter out material deemed inappropriate for children and to access only that which is suitable according to his or her own values. All major online services offer filtering, and ISPs serving 85 percent of all Internet users offer at least one form of filtering software. In addition, 241 local ISPs in over 35 states offer filtering software for free or at nominal cost.[3] You can find an extensive listing of ISPs in the United States that offer software solutions, including what solutions are available to subscribers, at http://www.netparents.org.

Steve Case, President of America Online, says:

> We are—today, right now—delivering tools that empower families, neighbors and educators to limit and filter what can be seen by and sent to our children. . . . And we realize many parents are intimidated by technology, so we've worked hard to make these parental control tools easy to use. . . . Our message to parents is clear: You shouldn't let your kids travel in cyberspace without parental controls.[4]

One survey shows that parents of Internet households would be less likely to cancel the Internet (7 percent) if their child downloads pornography than parents of non-Internet households (23 percent).[5] When asked what they would do if they discovered their child had downloaded sexually explicit material from the Internet, most parents said they would be hesitant to pull the plug. The majority indicated that they would most likely either obtain restrictive software or step up parental supervision. This indicates to me that cybersavvy parents may feel comfortable with new technologies and, therefore, more confident that they can implement the tools that fit the criteria for their home.

In this chapter I want to help you become comfortable with the tools available to you and your family. I also want to encourage you to choose the tools that are right for *your* "digital toolbox." Admittedly this technical information may be difficult to grasp at first. It's sort of like learning a foreign language. But keep pressing forward. The language of computers, the Internet, and software solutions will soon become a natural part of your vocabulary as you read and implement this wonderful new technology.

As you examine the tools described in this chapter, keep in mind your own criteria for protecting your child. Start a list of options that fit your family's needs and begin to build your own digital toolbox. Hopefully, by the end of the chapter, you'll have an idea of which tools you want to implement in your home. Please note that the information given here is based on product information provided by the various companies that make the tools. I have not reviewed all the tools and am not endorsing them. Before deciding on which tool is best for your family, you may want to refer to the reviews and evaluations of tools found in various consumer reports or at such Internet sites as www.kidshield.com.

Your Own Digital Toolbox

The beauty of building your own digital toolbox is that it can be customized to meet your unique needs because of the diversity of solutions from which you get to choose. You will be able to select the tool (or combination of tools) that will help you provide a safe online experience for your child, depending on your parenting goals, your relation-

FamilyPC Magazine Survey Results (www.familypc.com)

In 1997 *FamilyPC* magazine asked 750 parents about family life online. Here's what parents said:

- 68 percent were concerned that their children were accessing sexually explicit material on the Internet.
- 67 percent were concerned with marketing on the Internet to children.
- 26 percent use the parental controls offered by their ISP; only 4 percent use parental control software they had to buy, install, and maintain on their own.
- 27 percent said they allow their children to chat. Among parents who let their kids chat online, 68 percent try to monitor their children's exchanges.
- Nearly 78 percent of those surveyed said they "always know" what their kids are doing and where they're going because they watch them while they're online.[6]

ship with your child, the level of protection needed, and the amount of flexibility you desire. In appendix B you will find descriptions of tools that promote safe online experiences for children. You may want to explore these products in their entirety at their Web sites to determine which tools or tool combinations best fit your criteria.

You may be feeling like Susan and Tom—bewildered by all your options. Here are a few scenarios of tool implementation based on certain criteria that many parents have determined to be necessary for their homes. All of the following approaches should be partnered with your house rules—that you developed in chapter 5—building a trust relationship with your child, monitoring your child's online time, and spending time with your child online.

Don't be discouraged by terminology that may be new to you. It will be explained later in the chapter.

Scenario 1—The Simplest Solution: One-Stop Shopping

I'm completely computer and Internet illiterate. I don't have a clue which tool to use. What's the simplest solution I can choose with the least amount of worry?

If this is your situation, I would suggest that you choose either an ISP that offers parental controls or an ISP with server-based solutions that automatically block inappropriate content (see Clean ISPs chart in this chapter). Both options offer parents a one-stop shopping approach.

Choosing to use parental controls provided by your service provider will give greater parental customizability as opposed to a clean ISP, but this choice may not provide your child with as much access to the Internet as a server-based solution. Some ISPs and online services allow you to opt out of the protected system with an adult password. If your child needs or wishes to access content online, which may be blocked at the server, the flexibility of a password allows you to opt out of the closed system to surf the Net with your child.

Clean ISPs offering server-based solutions are less likely to be circumvented by a computer-savvy child and are usually updated at the server, putting less pressure on you. Remember, however, that most blocking software—even when it is implemented at the server—cannot completely block inappropriate content. If your child will be online when you're not present, be sure your child understands and complies with your house rules.

Scenario 2—The Safe and Secure Solution

I want the simplest solution but I can't be present all the time when my child is online. How can I make sure my child's online experience is 100 percent safe?

Currently the only way to achieve 100 percent safety is through a closed secure system. Unlike filters or blocking software, closed systems allow children access only to those preselected Internet sites that have been determined appropriate for children. Unlike filtering or blocking software, closed systems lock *children* out of the Internet rather than locking *inappropriate content on the Internet* away from children. EdView's Family Edition is an excellent choice for this solution.

Note: A closed system is 100 percent safe as long as the system is activated. Always remember, a computer-savvy kid can disengage any of the software tools.

Some parental control features, such as America Online's Kids Only, are also closed systems.

Scenario 3—The Safe Yet Flexible Solution

I'm comfortable with implementing software solutions. How can I select the safest combination of solutions that allow a flexible approach?

You have many options from which to choose. You may want to install an end-user blocking/filtering software, such as X-Stop or Cyber Patrol, that allows you, the parent, to opt out for unrestricted Internet access. A number of end-user software solutions now allow for a tremendous level of flexibility to customize lists of approved and denied sites and to block chat rooms, e-mail, and USENET.

Certain server-based solutions, such as X-Stop and Bess, allow for maximum Internet access but allow a limited degree of customizability by the parent. Other server-based solutions, such as GuardiaNet allow tremendous flexibility to customize lists of approved and denied sites and to block chat rooms, e-mail, and USENET while still providing maximum Internet access without inappropriate content.

If your child is computer literate and has Internet savvy, you may want to layer your protection. A layering approach involves using various software solutions in tandem with one another. For example, in addition to implementing end-user software, such as SurfWatch, you may also choose an ISP or an online service that has server-based solutions in place. The server-based software would catch any inappropriate material that might seep through the end-user software, while providing a second layer of protection for your child. You can layer even further by using filtered search engines, such as Yahooligans! or Alta Vista.

Note: In addition to protecting your child from inappropriate content, most of the software solutions mentioned in the above scenarios offer features to block e-mail and chat rooms, both of which are often used by predators to contact children.

The next section will give you more specific information on these technologies and "actions" available to protect your children on the Internet.

Types of Actions

In their *Technology Inventory,* prepared for the 1997 Internet Online Summit: Focus on Children, Lorrie Cranor and Paul Resnick researched current technologies that promote safe online experiences for children and found that they generally offer six types of "actions" based on content labels or the characteristics of online content. They range from least restrictive (least amount of protection) to most restrictive (maximum control): These technologies may suggest, search, monitor, inform, warn, or block.[7] Using their categories and adapting their findings, I've listed the types of actions available to protect children online. You'll notice that some of the tools are given more than once, indicating that they offer more than one type of action to meet the various needs of parents.

Action: Suggest

Open System Suggested List

Many Web sites, pamphlets, books, and organizations endorse or suggest a list *(white list)* of sites with appropriate content for children. The suggested list of *open systems* includes: Yahooligans!, Microsystems Route 6–16, CyberYES list, The Internet Kids & Family Yellow Pages, and Scholastic Network. It's important to remember that when child-safe and appropriate sites are recommended, yet not protected within a closed system, your child may be only a few hot links or clicks away from inappropriate or pornographic content. Children may be safe while exploring the suggested sites but they would not necessarily be protected once they have exited the site. One way to deal with this risk is to use an open list of suggested sites in tandem with blocking or filtering software. Bonus.com is an example of a list of "super sites" for kids that also offers a filter, NetScooter, to limit kids to prequalified terrain.

Cover art taken from *The Internet Kids and Family Yellow Pages*, 2nd ed., by Jean Armour Polly; ISBN: 0-07-882340-4; copyright 1997 by The McGraw-Hill Companies. Used with permission from Osborne/McGraw-Hill. For more information or to order this book, call 1-800-227-0900, or visit www.osborne.com.

> **White List:** Suggested and/or approved sites for children.
> **Suggested List for Open System:** White list of sites, not contained within a secure system, approved for children.
> **Suggested List for Closed System:** White list of sites, protected within a closed, secure system and approved for children.

Closed System Suggested List

Another type of *suggest* action is a white list contained within a closed system. Such systems differ from open systems in that the recommended or suggested content has been assimilated into its own partitioned and secure space.

Closed systems, while limiting access to the Internet, are probably the safest way for children to explore content pre-retrieved from the Net because they are the most restrictive tools available. They provide children with specific Web sites that often are rated and categorized by maturity level and quality, forming a network. Within a closed system, children cannot go beyond the network white list of approved Web sites. Closed systems are provided by on-line services or by brand name sites. Examples include Kids Only (a service of AOL) and Edview's Family Edition and Disneyblast.com to which you subscribe. Some technologies offer password options to disarm the closed system any time a parent wants his or her child to have access to the entire unfiltered Internet. Some filtering technologies also include lists of recommended sites for children to explore.

Action: Search

Internet search engines are software programs that allow people to enter a query and search all the indexed content that matches that query, using a string of words or phrases. The search typically provides a list of links to sites that correspond in some way to the topic searched. Searches can point the user to all types of content, including pornographic material. The good news is that some search engines can be configured to filter the query matches and show the user only those family-friendly matches that are appropriate for children. Alta Vista Filtered Search Service is an excellent tool designed to retain the global nature of the Internet while allowing users to search and filter the Web based on their own values. Other search engines, such as Yahooligans! (an Internet search engine for children), limit their searches to databases that contain only sites with content appropriate for children. Though filtered searches are not 100 percent safe, these search engines (available through your Internet browser) are wonderful tools to add to your digital toolbox. (An interesting note: The president of Alta Vista shared with those of us attending the 1997 Internet Online Summit: Focus on Children that he never allows his children to surf the Net without his supervision.)

Action: Monitor

Some products and services monitor and track only incoming communications, while others log both incoming and outgoing communications. Tools that monitor outgoing communications can often be configured to prevent your child from giving out personal information, such as a home address or phone number, that could be used to harm the child.

Some tools record a list of the content the user accesses or attempts to access for later inspection. The tool may record a complete log of sites accessed or include only sites with content deemed inappropriate for children. For example, Cyber Snoop logs all Internet activity while your child is online. You may review the log to determine which Web sites your child visited, what e-mail your child sent, or what kinds of chats your child was involved in. To maintain your trust relationship, it's a good idea to tell your child that you are monitoring him or her. Another filtering program, Net Nanny, optionally logs all attempts to access content in violation of your policy. Other examples of software that has monitoring capability include: Bess, CyberSentinel, CYBERsitter, GuardiaNet, I-Gear, Net Rated, and Smart-Filter.

Action: Inform

Some inform tools are designed to provide information about content whenever a user begins to access that content. *PICS (Platform for Internet Content Selection)* labels (more on this later in the chapter), reviews, and other descriptions of content can help you guide your child to what is appropriate. However, in order for this information to be useful, it must be easily accessible. For example, this information may be displayed in the form of a graphic or banner on a Web page, or as part of a browser or other software. EvaluWeb displays a banner indicating the age appropriateness of content as part of the corresponding Web pages.

Action: Warn

Like tools that inform, warning tools provide information about content. However, warning tools recommend not accessing content *before it is displayed.* These tools are useful in protecting children from accidentally downloading inappropriate content. Many adult Web sites include a prominent warning on an introductory page that content on other pages at the site are inappropriate for those under eighteen. Some include devices to make sure those under eighteen cannot access their content, but many rely on the warning as the only deterrent, which is not only insufficient but may be enticing to a curious child. A tool such as the Microsoft Internet Explorer Content Advisor, which is designed to block content but also includes a password override, could be used as a warning mechanism as well. You could provide a password that your child could use to access content that would otherwise be blocked. Thus your child would be warned that the content may not be appropriate, but he or she could proceed to access it anyway with your permission.

Action: Block/Filter

Blocking/filtering software prevents children from accessing inappropriate content. Some tools use word filters to screen out inappropriate content by preventing access to sites containing specific words. For example, filtering the word *breast* may prevent access to many pornographic sites. On the other hand, it may also filter out all sites that contain chicken breast recipes. Many of the earliest versions of parental control software used only word filters. Since this method goes *beyond* blocking inappropriate content, many new products as well as recent versions of existing products have begun actual site blocking in addition to word filters. This means that individual sites are reviewed and then the site's Internet address is blocked. This allows the user to access the chicken breast recipe, but those sites that contain content unsuitable for children are blocked. Zachary Britton, author of *SafetyNet: Guiding and Guarding Your Children on the Internet,* of-

Enough Is Enough
Filtering/Blocking Solutions for Technology Toolbox

	Cyber Patrol	CYBERsitter	GuardiaNet	Net Nanny	Net-Rated	SurfWatch	X-Stop	EdView	Bascom
Filter or closed system?	filter	filter	filter	filter	filter	filter		closed curriculum	closed curriculum
Mac version	yes	no	in development	no	in development	yes	yes	yes	yes
Chat block		yes	yes	yes	in development	yes	yes		
Foul words blocked: incoming	no	yes	yes	yes	yes	yes	yes		
outgoing	yes	yes	yes	yes	yes	no	yes		
Sites blocked: porn	yes	yes	yes	yes	yes	yes	yes	yes	yes
cults	yes		yes	yes	yes	yes	yes	yes	yes
hate speech	yes	yes	yes	yes	yes	yes	yes	yes	yes
dangerous (bombs, etc.)	yes	yes	yes	yes	yes	yes	yes	yes	yes
other	yes	yes	yes	yes	yes	yes	yes	yes	yes
E-mail block: incoming	no	yes—word content	yes	no	yes	no	no		
incoming attachments	no	yes	yes	no	yes	no	yes		
outgoing	yes	yew—word content	yes	yes	yes	no	no		
Library of sites	yes—30,000/10 days	yes—45,000	yes	yes—10,000	yes—15,000	yes—70,000	no	yes	yes
Editable: age levels	yes	no	yes	white list for kids	no	white list for kids	no	age-appropriate	age-appropriate
objectionable words	no		yes		yes	yes	yes		
objectionable sites	yes	yes	yes	yes	yes	yes	yes		
Monitor activities	corporate version	yes	yes	yes	yes—full report	no	no		
Control: amount of time	yes		yes	in development	yes	no	no		
time of day	yes		yes	in development	yes	no	no		
activities (CD-ROMS, etc.)	no	yes	no	yes	yes	no	no		
end-user level	yes	yes	no	yes	yes	no	yes		
server level	yes	yes	yes	some	no	yes	yes	yes	yes
Browser: Explorer	yes	yes	yes	yes	yes	yes	yes		
Netscape	yes	yes	yes	yes	yes	yes	yes		
Tamper resistant	yes	yes	yes	yes	yes	yes	yes	yes	yes
Phone	1-800-828-2808	1-800-388-2761	1-800-952-2452	1-800-340-7177	1-800-404-9913	1-800-458-6600	1-888-STOPXXX	612-338-0533	
Web site	www.cyberpatrol.com	www.solidoak.com	www.guardianet.net	www.netnanny.com	www.netrated.com	www.surfwatch.com	www.xstop.com	www.edview.com	www.bascom.com

Information provided by software companies. May be reprinted provided credit is given to Enough Is Enough.
The Enough Is Enough name and logo are registered Trademarks.

fers advice on blocking/filtering software. Check out his Web site for more information: http://www.kidshield.com. Blocking/filtering software can be categorized as server-based or end-user solutions. End-user solutions indicate that the software is installed on your own personal computer. You can use this software to block incoming information or e-mail, and some offer the option of blocking outgoing material as well. Some products will allow you to set different levels of protection for different children. Examples of end-user blocking/filtering tools are: Cyber Patrol, Cyber Sentinel, CYBERsitter, Cyber Snoop, Net Nanny, Net Rated, Net Shepherd, SurfWatch, and X-Stop.

Server-based blocking or filtering technology occurs when parental controls or filters are installed at the server level (ISP or third-party server), not on your computer. When the filtering is done as part of a network's normal Internet routing, it is effective throughout the entire network and is not prone to tampering by children at their personal computers.[8] Clean ISPs, for instance, attempt to block all inappropriate material as it passes through their servers, making it unnecessary to install filtering software on your computer. While you don't have to worry about updating lists or configuring software, some server-based solutions cannot be customized by the end-user.[9] Server-based solutions include AME, GuardiaNet, I-Gear, N2H2 (Bess), NetFilter, EdView, X-Stop's Shadow, and WebSENSE.

Many major online services offer blocking features integrated into their software. Other tools, like Microsoft Internet Explorer, filter or block content or specific Web sites based on any set of PICS labels or ratings chosen by the parent. Unfortunately it is impossible to block all pornographic Web sites and newsgroups due to the thousands of new sites being added to the Internet every week. In addition, Web sites that have been rated at one time may later change their content or move from one location to another.

New Developments

Clean Screen

CleanScreen Corporation offers powerful and flexible server-based filtering, which provides the end-user with a wide range of personal choices including a high degree of customizability, dynamic filter updates, and a news filter, e-mail filter, and clipping service. (www.cleanscreen.net)

BioPassword

Net Nanny Software International Inc. is developing a new security-related technology called BioPassword, which is based on keystroke dynamics, known as biometrics. BioPassword can algorithmically measure each individual's personal keystroke rhythm and develop a password signature. Even if your child discovers your password, he or she cannot replicate the required biometric signature pattern and will not be able to use it to gain access to a site.

Smart Cards

GuardiaNet has developed a smart card with which parents choose whatever controls they want for each child. There is a "token" associated with each child's account. This token can be kept on your hard drive or it can become portable by saving it to a floppy disk or a smart card.

A smart card is the size of a credit card with a wafer-thin chip embedded. When children go to school or to the library, they can check to see if the institution has a GuardiaNet subscription. If so, they just use their own smart cards, and away they go, protected by their parents' own Internet choices.

Where Tools Can Be Located

Lorrie F. Cranor and Paul Resnick report that the technologies needed to implement these six actions may be located on your personal computer, your online service, a third-party *(remote proxy)* server, a *local area network (LAN)* or local proxy server or they may be part of a search engine or Web site.

Your Personal Computer

You can configure some of these tools on your personal computer (PC). (Instructions for doing this will be in the tool you choose.) Your computer-savvy children may reconfigure or disengage the tool against your wishes and possibly without your knowledge. Some PC-based products have been designed with mechanisms to prevent tampering. Many PC-based products require frequent updates and some can update themselves automatically when the PC is connected to the Internet.

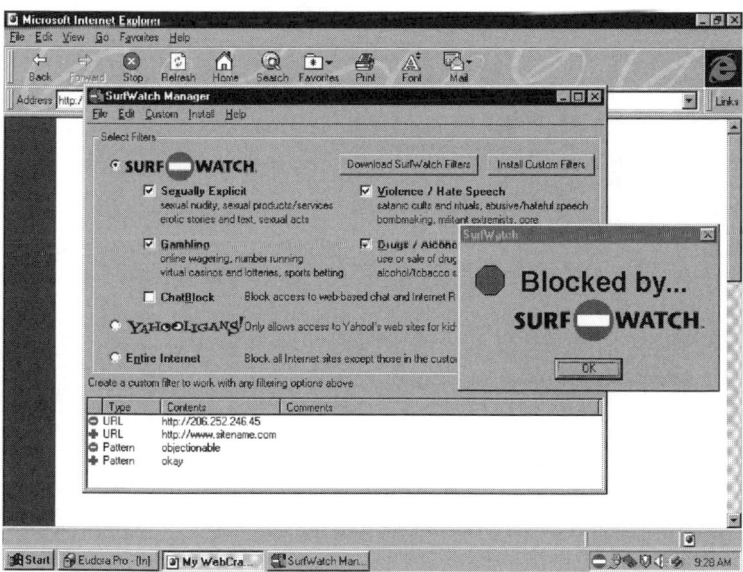

SurfWatch, which can be installed on your personal computer, offers users filtering choices.

Online Service Providers

Some service providers offer a variety of parental controls, including site blocking, limitation on receipt of e-mail, and restricted access to chat rooms, newsgroups, or other types of services. These are available at no cost and are easy to configure as part of establishing children's accounts. Server-based parental controls, such as America Online's Kids Only Area, create clean channels suitable for kids, yet those controls are not integrated throughout the entire online service. Clean ISPs, on the other hand, block or filter content through their entire network. FlashNet, the largest privately held ISP in the nation, announced in early 1998 that it will restrict all access to online pornography. Others may offer clean service as one of their product offerings. Tools that can be run by an ISP include: AME, GuardiaNet, CleanScreen, SurfWatch, X-Stop, and WebSENSE.

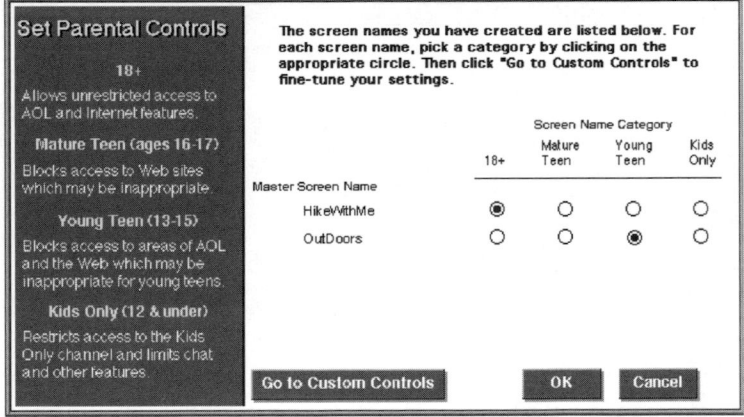

Many Online Services have parental-control features in place that serve as a starting point for many families. On America Online, for example, the controls range from "kids only" to "young teens" and "mature teens," as well as controls to block e-mail, instant messages, and chat rooms.

Enough Is Enough
Clean Internet Service Providers

	Berean Solutions	CleanNet	DTN	FamilyConnect	Family Online
Cost per month	$21.95	$19.95	$19.95	$23.95	$19.95
Mac version	yes	yes	yes	no	yes
Chat available	no	limited	no	yes	available
Chat block available		yes		yes	
Instant/private messages available	on Internet	yes	on Internet	coming	no
Instant/private message block	yes	no	no	no	
Foul words blocked: incoming	no	no	no	in chat	e-mail
outgoing	no	no	no	in chat	no
Sites blocked: porn	yes	yes	yes	yes	yes
cults	yes	yes	yes	yes	yes
hate speech	yes	yes	yes	yes	yes
dangerous (bombs, etc.)	yes	yes	yes	yes	yes
other potentially objectionable	yes	yes	yes	yes	yes
USENET newsgroup block	yes	yes	yes	coming	yes
E-mail block: incoming	yes	no	no	no	no
attachments	graphic				
outgoing	no	no	no	no	no
Editable: age levels	no	yes	yes	no	at server
Opt to unfiltered Internet access	no	yes	no	no	no
Monitor/log activities	log	log	yes	no	no
Control: amount of time	no	no	yes	no	no
time of day	no	yes	yes	no	no
Browser used: Netscape	yes	yes	yes	yes	yes
Explorer	yes	yes	yes	yes	yes
Regions	National	Canada/some U.S.	National	National	Southern California
Phone	1-888-277-9209	519-823-5100	1-388-432-1DTN	1-888-400-0434	626-792-6226
Web site	http://www.berean.net	http://cleannet.net	http://www.dtnhome.com	http://gofamily.com	http://www.fam.net

Information provided by Internet Service Providers. May be reprinted provided credit is given to Enough Is Enough. The Enough Is Enough name and logo are registered trademarks.

	Illumanet	Integrity Online	Maranatha	Mayberry USA	Rated G
Cost per month	$24.95	$19.95	$20.00	$29.95	$24.95
Mac version	no	yes	yes	yes	yes
Chat available	no	no	no	yes	coming
Chat block available				yes	
Instant/private messages available	no	yes	no	yes	no
Instant/private message block				no	
Foul words blocked: incoming	yes	no	yes	no	yes
outgoing	yes	no	yes	no	no
Sites blocked: porn	yes	yes	yes	yes	yes
cults	yes	yes	yes	yes	yes
hate speech	yes	yes	yes	yes	yes
dangerous (bombs, etc.)	yes	yes	yes	yes	yes
other potentially objectionable	yes	yes	yes	yes	yes
USENET newsgroup block	yes	yes	yes	yes	yes
E-mail block: incoming	yes	no	yes	yes	yes
attachments	no		graphics	no	
outgoing	yes	no	yes	no	no
Editable: age levels	no	yes	no	yes	no
opt to unfiltered Internet access	yes	no	yes	no	no
Monitor activities	yes	no	no	no	no
Control: amount of time	yes	no	log	no	no
time of day	yes	no	yes	no	no
Browser used: Netscape	yes	yes	yes	yes	yes
Explorer	own version	yes	own version	yes	yes
Regions	International	National	National	National and Canada	National
Phone	1-888-455-8626	503-649-3001	1-888-466-2683	1-888-629-2379 x 2015	1-888-711-6381
Web site	http://illuma.net	http:www.Integrityonline.com	http://maranatha.net	http://www.mayberryusa.net	http://www.rated-g.com

Information provided by Internet Service Providers. May be reprinted provided credit is given to Enough Is Enough. The Enough Is Enough name and logo are registered trademarks.

Third-Party (Remote Proxy) Servers

Online services or Internet Access Providers sometimes offer this type of service where parental controls or filters are installed at a remote facility, not on your computer. In addition, some software companies offer their software solutions via their own servers. You may subscribe to a third-party service, even if your ISP doesn't offer one.

Subscribers to third-party servers configure their browser software to pass all requests through the remote server. Some of these services include tools that prevent children from defeating the controls. Third-party servers are useful because they may be continuously updated at the remote server, and you won't have to download the latest list of "forbidden sites" to your home computer. They may also have more security since your child can't tamper with them locally. Make sure you select one with flexibility that provides for different configurations for different family members, while allowing you to set up your own list of allowed and denied sites. Third-party servers include: Bess, GuardiaNet, I-Gear, EdView, PlanetView, and WebSENSE.

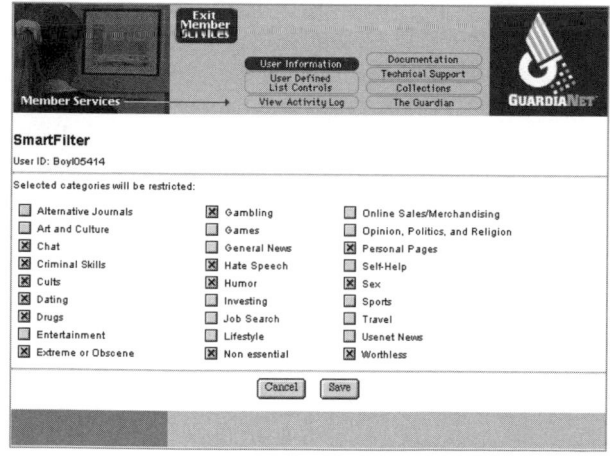

GuardiaNet, a server-based solution, offers parents both high configurability and low maintenance.

Local Area Networks (LANs) or Local Proxy Servers

You probably don't have a LAN in your home, but implementing tools on LANs using local proxy servers can be a useful solution for networked PCs in schools and libraries. These work the same as third-party servers, but the filter is located at the institution's own server, not at a third party's server. Centralized configuration is sometimes easier for system administrators to handle and harder for individuals to defeat. Tools that can be run on LANs or local proxy servers include: Bess, X-Stop, Cyber Patrol, Cyber Snoop, I-Gear, Net Nanny, SafeSurf Internet Filtering Solution, SmartFilter, and SurfWatch.

Search Engines

Some search engines offer Internet search services that return only results that are appropriate for children. For example, Net Shepherd has teamed with the Alta Vista search engine so that children can search the Web and access only those sites that meet rating criteria specified by parents. Other "safe search" examples include Yahooligans! and N2H2.

Web Sites

Many Web sites list content that is appropriate for children, for example, Yahooligans!, Bonus.com, and www.netmom.com. Other Web sites contain PICS labels, graphics, or other descriptions of their content that can be useful to parents in guiding their children. EvaluWEB provides both PICS labels and banner graphics indicating the age-appropriateness of Web sites.

More about Tools and Rating Systems: Making Choices

Customizing Tools

Internet blocking/filtering tools have a large range of customization options including:

- the ability to allow approved sites (white lists) and block unapproved sites (black lists)
- the targeting of key words and/or phrases to trigger actions
- the designation of whole categories of content to allow or block
- the choice of whether inappropriate content should trigger a block, a warning message, a log entry, or other actions
- the capacity to make different configurations for different children in your household

Platform for Internet Content Selection (PICS)

PICS provides computer code specifications or a common language for labeling material on the Web. Developed by the World Wide Web Consortium (an industry consortium that develops common standards for the Web and is backed by many of the largest online commercial companies), PICS allows your Web browsers and/or a number of stand-alone filtering products (such as CyberPatrol) to screen sites based on their content ratings, allowing access only to the sites bearing ratings you have selected. PICS does not set the rating standards or rate the sites. Rather it enables the creation of *rating services*, filtering products, and other software that take action based on content that is self-labeled and/or labeled by third parties. Not all of the technological tools available use PICS specifications. However, when a filtering product is PICS compatible, the product is able to read any label that is in the PICS specified format.

Recreational Software Advisory Council on the Internet (RSACi) and SafeSurf are examples of independent rating systems that are designed for self-rating by any content provider. By default, Microsoft's Internet Explorer 4.0 Web browser uses RSACi's rating system, but the other third-party rating systems may also be used. Selecting this software means your children can access only a very few sites because so few sites have been rated at all and, of those, only a few are rated "good." Three PICS-based labeling services, including RSACi and SafeSurf, have rated more than 300,000 sites around the world; however, limiting access to only preapproved sites may seriously restrict your child's access to all the healthy data of the Internet.[10]

PICS is a Herculean attempt to provide a self-regulating Internet mechanism. It is my belief that until Internet-rated content hits critical mass (i.e., the vast majority of content gets rated as opposed to most content remaining unrated, as currently), filtering based on a PICS rating system will continue to remain limited.

For more information about PICS, you may want to consult appendix F: PICSRules.

How Content Gets Classified

Before you begin building your digital toolbox, you need to understand who (or what kind of automated tool) is classifying Internet content and what criteria is being used in the technology you have chosen to use. Classifying content may be done by content providers, third-party experts, parents, through surveys or votes, and by automated tools.

- Content providers: RSACi and SafeSurf are examples of PICS rating systems designed to be used by content providers.
- Third-party experts: Filtering companies, such as AME, Bess, Bonus.com, Cyber Patrol, and SurfWatch, use teams of information specialists, parents, and teachers to assist in classifying content.
- Local administrators: A parent, teacher, or other "administrator" can decide what type of content should be accessible to children under his or her supervision.
- Survey or vote: Net Shepherd has established a "rating community" of people who rate and classify content.
- Automated tools: Some companies, such as EvaluWEB, have developed automated tools to classify content as the user requests it. Other software that employs automated tools include CYBERsitter, NetFilter, and Net Nanny.[11]

The following entities have evaluated many of the blocking and filtering software solutions. Check out what they found:
Family PC http://www.familypc.com
Consumer Report http://www.consumerreports.com
KidShield http://www.kidshield.com

Net Nanny is one of the few software companies that make their list of blocked sites available to the public.

Other companies view their blocked lists as proprietary. The proprietary nature of the blocked lists fuels much of the First Amendment debate with respect to the use of blocking/filtering software, particularly in schools and libraries.

Classification schemes are designed to identify content that is "good for kids" and/or "bad for kids." It may be classified on the basis of:

- age appropriateness
- specific characteristics or elements of the content
- who created the content

With the appearance of more and more Web sites every day, new content must be classified so that software tools that utilize classification information can stay up to date. Some products and services are continuously updated and are easy for users to quickly update. Others require users to manually download updates. For information about third-party labeling services, check out appendix H: Third-Party Labels from Values-Oriented Organizations.

Questions to Ask Your Internet Service or Internet Access Provider

Try to imagine your child going to the park in your neighborhood and being approached by a pedophile, who has a way of knowing exactly when your son or daughter is playing there. Now imagine that this pedophile has invited his friends to the park to meet your child. This is the type of encounter that may take place online. Depending on your Internet Service Provider, your child's screen name may be found in a member listing or added to a list that announces your child's arrival online, and anyone can send your child private messages—even if your child has never entered a chat room.

You have the power to protect your child from such online activity. Here is a list of questions that you can address with your ISP or online service.[12]

- Do you have online profiles? Do you have a member directory? How can a parent keep a screen name or an account name unlisted?
- Do you have chat rooms? Are there specific chat rooms for minors? Are they monitored? Is there a mechanism in place to block chat rooms?
- Do you have some sort of private/instant message system? How do users block receiving private messages? Can users block only some, or is it all or nothing?
- Do you have an option (like a posted list or buddy list) that allows people online to see if others are online? Does it have a blocking system?
- Do you have a way to block e-mail from individual accounts or from certain addresses or types of sites? What about reporting unwanted e-mail?
- What other parental controls or protections for minors do you have available?
- How do users report suspicious online activity?

For a more comprehensive list of questions to ask filtering software companies, check out Net-mom Jean Armour Polly's suggestions at her Web site: http://www.netmom.com.

Still confused about what to put in your digital toolbox? Try rereading this chapter and read appendix B: Tool Descriptions. You may want to start with a small toolbox that contains a more restrictive solution, particularly if your child is very young or new to the Internet. Later, as you and your child become more experienced, you can move to a larger, more flexible toolbox.

Imagine your software tools to be your child's key to the vehicle that will carry him or her down the Information Superhighway. Just as you would prepare your child for his or her first driving experience, plan to teach your child the rules of Internet travel. It's a good idea to spend some time first traveling online with your child and then monitoring his or her online experience to rate your child's driving. As you gain confidence in the vehicle and in your child's trustworthiness, you will be able to delegate more and more flexibility and responsibility to your child, while implementing technological solutions that will bring peace of mind and assurance of a safe online experience for your child.

Cybersavvy Quiz #5

Take the following quiz to see how cybersavvy you are. Then review this chapter and use the glossary to get more specific information on areas that are confusing or unclear.

1. Technological solutions that address parents' concerns about Internet access offer which of the following actions?
   a. monitor
   b. block
   c. warn
   d. all of the above
2. PICS stands for:

    a. Platform for Internet Content Selection
    b. Program Internet Control Station
    c. Protocol Internet Control Solutions
    d. Party In Chat Space

3. Clean ISPs/OSPs:
   a. block inappropriate material from entering their services
   b. refuse to accept dirty language from their subscribers
   c. is a message that comes from your server telling you when to clean your computer for viruses
   d. are Web sites that are porn free

4. RSACi is an example of:
   a. an Internet ratings system
   b. a foreign Web address
   c. Palestinian cuisine
   d. a misspelled word

5. To find out more about your ISP, you should ask:
   a. Do you offer software solutions for kids' safety online?
   b. Do you have a way to block e-mail?
   c. How do users report suspicious online activity?
   d. all of the above

Scoring: If you chose answer A for questions 2, 3, and 4, and D for questions 1 and 5, you answered correctly. Congratulations! If you missed several answers, take some time to reread this chapter.

For further information on blocking and filtering tools, refer to the following resources and see appendices A, B, and F.

Safety Net: Guiding and Guarding Your Children on the Internet, Zachary Britton

A Parent's Guide to the Internet, Parry Aftab

Internet Online Summit Technology Inventory, Lorrie
Faith Cranor and Paul Resnick, at www.research
.att.com/projects/tech4kids. The Web site is regularly updated to reflect technology tools updates.

7

Expanding Your Child's Safety Net

Susan added another place setting to the table in the breakfast room before settling into a chair across from Tom.

"Tom, did you know that the school library has Internet access?" asked Susan, as she buttered a blueberry muffin.

Tom folded his newspaper and poured himself a bowl of Cheerios. "Since when?"

"I don't know, but yesterday when I picked up Lily, she told me that she didn't need to use the computer last night because she had already done the research for her social studies report online at the library."

"Well, that's great, I guess," Tom replied.

"But Tom, what about safety? Do you suppose the library is using any software tools like the ones we're using at home to protect kids from predators and keep them out of Web sites where they don't belong?"

"I suppose we'd better find out. Lily seems to be following our house rules, but I'm not too keen on the school or library allowing kids unrestricted Internet access."

"I wonder whether the teachers and librarian are supervising the kids who are going online," Susan commented. "Maybe we should ask Lily."

"Maybe you should ask me what?" asked Lily as she plopped down in the chair between her parents.

"Lily, has anyone in your class ever gone online without your teacher being in the room?"

Lily spooned some Cheerios into her mouth and nodded.

Susan and Tom exchanged concerned glances. Lily swallowed and said, "One of the kids from the sixth grade got caught the other day in the library looking at an X-rated site."

"Does your teacher or the librarian have any rules for going online?" asked Tom.

"Yes," replied Lily, "but some of the kids use the instant screen saver so when the librarian walks by, she can't tell that they're online."

"Maybe I should talk to your teacher or the principal," Susan remarked, "and find out if the school is using any safety tools. I don't want you to have an unsafe experience because one of your classmates isn't abiding by the rules."

Just as we want to ensure the safety of our children's online experiences at home, like Susan and Tom, we need to be concerned about our children's safety outside the home, particularly at school and the public library. If the safety measures discussed in previous chapters are not implemented in the classroom and in the library, our children are at risk. After all, 70 percent of children's Internet access occurs away from home.[1] While parental supervision is the first line of defense in the home, the same is not necessarily true or possible for classrooms and libraries.

In this chapter, I want to help you understand the issues surrounding school and library access to the Internet while equipping you to work with these institutions in order to implement policies and software solutions that will help to ensure that your child's Internet access is just as safe at school and the library as it is at home. For these institutions to properly address the needs of our children, parents must play an active role. In addition, each school and library should have clear policies regarding Internet access, and those policies should be proactively communicated to parents.

First Encounters

Schools and libraries are where many adults first encounter computers and online technology if they haven't already been forced to become computer literate at their job. Some parents are excited about the educational opportunities the Internet offers schools that may have limited or outdated libraries. Other parents are disturbed because they have heard only about the dangers. And many teachers and administrators have good reason to be concerned about the risks and liabilities of opening the Internet door to student use.

Libraries are often a community's primary location for information, research, and Internet access. Those of us who have fond memories of the positive role of libraries in our life have grown to trust enormously these institutions. Unfortunately the world has changed, and now more than ever, we cannot assume that everything we read is true. We now have to evaluate all forms of information for credible sources, accuracy, and appropriateness. Teaching discernment is one of our most important tasks as parents and child advocates.

As more and more schools and libraries add computer labs and classes to their facilities, more and more of those computers will be linked to the Internet. With President Clinton's goal to connect every classroom to the Internet by the year 2000, all schoolchildren will have access to the same universe of knowledge and the opportunity to acquire the skills they need to succeed in the high-tech workplace of the twenty-first century.[2]

Internet Access

- 78 percent of all U.S. public schools have at least one line connected to the Internet[3]
- 95 percent of all private schools are equipped with computers; 9 percent have Internet access[4]
- 5 percent of religious private schools have computers with Internet access[5]
- 31 percent of schools with a large proportion of students from poor families have access to the Internet, compared to 62 percent of schools with higher-income students[6]
- 27 percent of all instructional classrooms have Internet access (up from 14 percent last year)[7]
- 72.3 percent of all public libraries in the United States are connected to the Internet with about 60.4 percent of those libraries making their Internet access available for public use[8]

Pornography Access

Now for some more disturbing statistics. In a 1997 GRIP survey of students who have *unintentionally* downloaded pornography while surfing the Net:

- 22 percent downloaded it at their school Internet connection
- 25 percent downloaded it at their public library Internet connection

The percentage of students who have *intentionally* downloaded pornography while surfing the Net were:

- 16 percent at their school Internet connection
- 11 percent at their public library connection

Schools that are using this new technology are blazing the trail for our children's education and future. For example, students have considerably more enthusiasm for projects when they have access to recent and relevant information. Other benefits include direct access to experts, unpublished works, and video-conferencing. Students who are really engaged and interacting with material are more likely to dig deeper and retain what they learn. As I mentioned in chapter 1, computer assisted learning may prove to enhance academic performance while motivating hard-to-reach and learning-disabled students. Unquestionably this new technology can support teachers in customizing curriculum to meet the needs of individual students.

As Internet use increases in schools and libraries, however, a child's risk for exposure to harmful online content or activity increases as well. Consider the following examples:

- Roberta Bowman pulled her fifteen-year-old son out of his local high school and enrolled him in a private school after she discovered he used a classroom computer to view pornography on the Internet. Shocked, then angry, Mrs. Bowman complained, "When the schools open themselves up to the Internet without having any kind of prevention measures in place, they open themselves up to everything."[9]
- A high school teacher in Tennessee was suspended without pay for allegedly using school materials, equipment, and Internet service—on school time—to transmit and receive digital computer photographs and messages that exhibited explicit sex involving himself and others.[10]
- A forty-nine-year-old man was charged with the illegal use of a minor in nudity-oriented material after downloading pictures of nude boys at a public library in Lakewood, Ohio. Library officials banned the man from the library but said they won't change their policy, allowing users unrestricted Internet access.[11]
- A man whom librarians had never seen before recently monopolized a computer at the public library for hours surfing the Internet for pornography. Then he lured three young boys to the screen to watch the images. The librarians at this branch had little recourse but to watch helplessly as the man and boys gazed at the nude depictions.[12]

"Internet terminals in schools and libraries are being used to access pornography and other sexually explicit material approximately four times every minute, according to an analysis performed by N2H2™ Inc. on select schools and libraries in North America."[13] Many organizations are concerned about the availability of not only sexually explicit material but also games, sports information, hate speech, gambling sites, and other content that may be unsuitable to access during school hours.

In introducing the Internet School Filtering Act to Congress, Republican senator from Arizona John McCain suggests the following:

> Schools and libraries can select the technology that best suits their community standards. The prevention lies, not in censoring what goes onto the Internet, but rather in filtering what comes out of it onto the computers our children use outside the home. . . . We must tackle this problem of children innocently stumbling onto indecent material while using the web for legitimate research purposes or [we will] face dire consequences.

Unfortunately there is currently no consensus on the precise role of schools and libraries in structuring children's Internet access, nor is there consensus on the methods that should be employed. This lack of consensus concerns all public institutions in general and libraries in particular and revolves primarily around the question of whether such institutions should use software tools, such as blocking or filtering tools, or other approaches to limit children's access.

There has been, and continues to be, tremendous discussion over the library and school administration's role in providing safe Internet access. Some believe that parents, educators, and librarians have the responsibility to teach critical thinking skills to children, to show them which areas of cyberspace to steer clear of, and to fa-

miliarize them with the clues that a person they're talking to on the Internet (via e-mail or chat rooms) might
not be who he or she purports to be. The challenge for
school administrators, teachers, and librarians is that
the Internet was designed to *not* be controlled. Nevertheless, if we don't find a way to implement the necessary safeguards on the Internet in classrooms and libraries, the benefits of education and research will be
hard to realize.[14] Parents and child advocates want children to be safe no matter where they are.

Strategies for Schools and Libraries

Many of the strategies for protecting our children
when they're online at home can also be used to protect their online experiences at school and the library.
As these institutions connect to the Internet, I believe
they need to develop Internet acceptable-use policies
in addition to implementing technological tools to protect our children. These policies should require adult
supervision of students during online sessions, prohibit intentional viewing of sexually explicit or inappropriate material (as defined in the policies), and em-
ploy appropriate measures to protect children from
such material.

Unfortunately many schools and libraries follow the
American Library Association's recommendation to
provide unfiltered access on the Internet, regardless of
the age of students. Others are implementing software
tools. Before a policy is chosen by these institutions
parents should have the opportunity to evaluate it. It is
up to *you, the parents,* to understand the implications
of unrestricted access. You have the right to play a role
in your children's use of the Internet while at school or
at the library.

Supervision

A computer with access to the Internet should be located in a classroom or library where the supervising adult has the best chance of viewing the screen. School computers should be placed along walls of the classroom with the monitors facing the center of the room so the teacher can glance about and make sure all students are safely surfing.[15] In a library the computer should be located where it can be viewed by the library staff. When an adult supervisor leaves the area for an extended time, Internet access can be shut down.

In their "Technology Inventory," Lorrie Cranor and Paul Resnick suggest that the configuration for computers used in public spaces should be changed frequently. For example, when computers are used in a classroom science lesson, the teacher may provide access only to science-related Web sites, but later that day, the same computers may be available for more general research. Similarly, in libraries, some patrons may prefer to work on computers with filters while others prefer working with ratings software. Software vendors, say Cranor and Resnick, are beginning to respond to this need, but users should encourage software vendors to allow flexible configurations in *all* software tools.[16]

"Hold Harmless" Agreements

Some schools and libraries have chosen to "pass the buck" of Internet responsibility to parents with absurd "hold harmless" agreements. These agreements ask parents to hold the school or library harmless of any liability in the event their son or daughter is exposed to risks online while at school or the library. Many schools that send these letters home for parental signature deny

Internet access to any student who has not received his
or her parents' written permission. On the surface, this
may seem responsible, but in many cases, these same
schools have not implemented software solutions to help
ensure that their students' Internet access is safe and
educational. Furthermore, I doubt that such schools are
giving parents full disclosure regarding the risks of unrestricted Internet access. Parents can use the Sample
Letter Requesting Safe Internet Access below as a response to hold-harmless agreements.

The bottom-line choice for parents in such instances
is to either deny their children Internet access while at
school or the library or risk very real dangers to their
children by allowing unrestricted Internet access. The
preferred choice is for parents to work with their children's schools and libraries to develop an appropriate
Internet use policy and technology plan, which incor-
porate software that screens out inappropriate content.
Schools are often open to this type of involvement from
concerned parents. Once such plans are implemented,
parents will feel more comfortable and confident in allowing their children to access the Internet while at
school or at the library.

Sample Letter Requesting
Safe Internet Access

Attn:

I appreciate the opportunity for children to use the
Internet for research and educational purposes. I would
be abdicating my responsibility as a parent, however, if
I signed an Internet Use Policy without knowing that
protection from Internet dangers is firmly in place for
my child and other children. Those of us responsible for

the safety of children must recognize there are two clear and present dangers to children on the Internet: (1) online predators' easy access to children, and (2) children's easy access to pornography.

The Internet is widely recognized by law enforcement as the pedophile's playground. Sexual predators search for children online, exploiting them by exposing them to pornography and luring them into offline meetings. These predators utilize chat rooms, private messaging, and e-mail to gain the trust of children in order to later harm them.

In addition to facing sexual predators, children also face an enormous amount of pornography online. Recent data estimates that there are more than ninety-two thousand Web sites containing pornography that is illegal for both adults and children, which children can easily access both intentionally and unintentionally. These sites contain graphic, violent, and deviant images that have proven extremely damaging to children. Children also have access to pornography legal for adults, such as *Playboy/Penthouse*–type images, but illegal for children in both print and broadcast media.

My understanding is that one of the ways children can be protected online is through the utilization of blocking technology which, although not 100 percent effective, serves as a protective measure. Another mechanism which *is* 100 percent effective is a closed Internet system.

I am not willing to exempt this institution from liability until you can assure me that precautions have been taken to keep children safe when on the Internet. I realize that by refusing to sign your permission letter, my child will be denied Internet access.

Like other concerned parents, I do not want my child to be at a disadvantage. I want my child to benefit from the wonderful opportunities provided by Internet access. If you have installed protective measures to your Internet access, such as blocking or a closed curriculum, please let me know. If you have not, I urge you and the governing board to make the protection of children in this regard a top priority. Once you have taken action to ensure the safety of our children online, please let me know, so I can allow my child Internet access while at your institution.

Sincerely,[17]

Acceptable-Use Policies

Many state departments of education and local school districts have recommended that schools and libraries develop a contract with every student who goes online at these institutions. Even with the installation of software solutions, a library or school needs to make clear the responsibilities and privileges of each Internet user. Some examples of Internet acceptable-use policies follow.

Baltimore County Public Schools
Telecommunications Acceptable Use Policy for Students

Purpose of Telecommunications

Telecommunications extend the classroom beyond the school building by providing access to information resources on local, state, national, and international electronic networks such as the Internet. For students, telecommunications use in the Baltimore County Public Schools is for educational purposes, such as accessing curriculum-related information, sharing resources, and promoting innovation in learning. Learning how to use this wealth of information and how to communicate electronically are information literacy skills which support student achievement and success in the 21st century.

Information Available

- Government publications and databases
- Museums and art galleries
- Maps and other geographic resources
- Encyclopedias and dictionaries
- Magazines and newspapers
- Library catalogs and community directories

Telecommunications Safety

Precautions will be taken to attempt to ensure that the Internet is a safe learning environment. Students will be supervised while using the Internet and will be instructed in the appropriate and safe use, selection, and evaluation of information. Also, software which attempts to block access to objectionable material will be accessible on computer networks used by students.

Terms and Conditions

Students shall:

✓ Use telecommunications for educational purposes only.

✓ Communicate with others in a courteous and respectful manner.

✓ Maintain the privacy of personal name, address, phone number, password, and respect the same privacy of others.

✓ Use only telecommunication accounts and passwords provided by the school.

✓ Report any incident of harassment to the supervising employee.

✓ Comply with copyright laws and intellectual property rights of others.

Students shall not:

✗ Knowingly enter unauthorized computer networks to tamper or destroy data.

✗ Access or distribute abusive, harassing, libelous, obscene, offensive, profane, pornographic, threatening, sexually explicit, or illegal material.

✗ Install personal software on computers.

✗ Use telecommunications for commercial, purchasing, or illegal purposes.

Disclaimer

The accuracy and quality of the information cannot be guaranteed. No warranties for telecommunications access are expressed or implied; BCPS will not be responsible for any information that may be lost, damaged, or unavailable due to technical or other difficulties.

Penalties

Violations of the Telecommunications Acceptable Use Policy may be a violation of law, civil regulations, or Board Policies 5550, 5570, or 5660. Suspension of telecommunications privileges, school disciplinary action, and/or legal action may result from infringement of this policy.

Baltimore County Public Schools
Student Handbook Acknowledgment Form

This form must be signed and dated by the student and his/her parent/guardian after reviewing the Handbook. The student will return the completed form to the school.

School:_____

_____	_____	_____
Last Name (PLEASE PRINT)	First Name (PLEASE PRINT)	Grade

I have received a copy of the *Baltimore County Public Schools Student Handbook.* The Handbook was explained, and I was given the opportunity to ask questions. Particular attention was paid to the disciplinary code listed in the book, and the consequences for all offenses were clearly stated. Additionally, I understand the *Telecommunications Acceptable Use Policy.* I was informed that I could meet individually with an assistant principal to discuss the book in more detail.

_____   _____

Student's Signature   Date

I have discussed this Handbook with my child. I have reviewed the *Telecommunications Acceptable Use Policy* and understand that if I do not want my child to participate in the use of telecommunications I will attach a letter to this form and return it to the principal.

_____   _____

Parent's/Guardian's Signature   Date

RETURN FORM WITHIN FIVE SCHOOL DAYS

Note: *In this policy, students have the responsibility for appropriate online behavior, and the Baltimore County Public School system attempts to ensure Internet safety by providing software solutions and adult supervision.*

Problems with Internet Use Policies

While most of these Internet use policies encourage responsible behavior by students, teachers, librarians, and administrators in accordance with a code of conduct, some neglect to address the following illegal activities:

- selling drugs or other illegal materials online
- using copyrighted material without permission
- creating or distributing computer viruses
- using somebody else's name or code number to send or receive messages
- sending racist, sexist, inflammatory, or obscene messages
- "hacking" of any kind

When evaluating a school's or library's Internet use policy, don't forget to check on the consequences for failure to abide by the rules. In some policies, breaking the rules results in suspension of computer privileges or even prosecution.

Software Solutions

Historically library purchases have been limited by funds, shelving, and carefully drafted selection policies. The Internet is considered outside these selection policies in many libraries. Yet it gives access to some materials not commonly found in public libraries, ranging from references and unpublished works to illegal pornography. While many libraries report no problems with this, others have experienced incidents where materials that were downloaded and printed caused serious concern to patrons or employees.[18]

As schools and libraries struggle with the safety issues of Internet access, there is a growing interest in the implementation of software solutions, especially in schools. Software companies, as well as educational groups like Enough Is Enough, are working to make teachers, administrators, and librarians aware of the various software tools available and suitable for schools and libraries.

There has been a tremendous and heated debate over the issue of libraries implementing software solutions. Although installation of software technology may seem to be a simple solution, there is no consensus on whether libraries should use such technology to limit children's Internet access. Some believe that this would be constitutionally inappropriate if anything other than illegal materials are blocked. Others argue that filtering is merely an extension of the selection process.

Some of the concerns are valid. For example, I believe it is within the librarian's purview to implement flexible and customizable software, minimizing dependence on third parties to determine which content should be blocked. The newer generations of software put the control of content selection in the hands of the librarian.

On the other hand, I believe that librarians, as information providers in the community, must accept their responsibility to protect children from exposure to material that in any other media would be considered illegal for children to access (i.e., obscenity, child pornography, and material "harmful to minors"). Furthermore, when libraries refuse to accept this responsibility, I believe they should give full disclosure to parents about the potential risks posed to children by unrestricted Internet access at the library. Unless parents understand the online risks to children, they will assume that their children are safe at the local public library. I also believe that libraries should not provide adults with access to

Internet content that is illegal, even for adults, such as child pornography and obscenity (see chapter 3 for information on types of pornography).

> An April 1998 article from the Associated Press said that it has been documented through the tracking logs of the Utah Education Network (UEN) that public school students tried to access pictures of naked women or other prohibited material 275,000 times in just one month. In February students tried more than 250,000 times to access Internet sites that were sexual in nature or dealt with sexuality. The filters used by UEN were successful in blocking most of the inappropriate sites, although it is impossible to block all unwanted material because new sites are added daily. Ninety percent of their school computers are hooked up to the filter, and the remaining 10 percent soon will be.

If your child's school or library is still grappling with their choices on selection and implementation of policy and tools, you as a parent have a tremendous opportunity to help shape these very important decisions in the early stages. By the time you finish this chapter, it is my hope that you will be equipped and confident in working with your child's school and library in this process.

ALA and ACLU on Filtering

The American Library Association has issued a formal statement, "Resolution on the Use of Filtering Software in Libraries," which concludes with the following:

> WHEREAS, the use of in libraries of software filters which block constitutionally protected speech is inconsistent with the United States Constitution and federal law and may lead to legal exposure for the library and its governing authorities; now, therefore, be it

RESOLVED, that the American Library Association affirms that the use of filtering software by libraries to block access to constitutionally protected speech violates the Library Bill of Rights.[19]

Librarians from around the country have reported that ALA antifiltering spokespersons are going to librarian conferences and workshops warning librarians about the legal consequences of filtering. At its annual convention in 1997, the ALA passed a resolution calling for unfiltered Internet access in the nation's libraries. Many ALA spokespeople also have standing ties to the American Civil Liberties Union (ACLU).

The ACLU's official position on pornography reveals their underlying agenda with respect to filtering or blocking pornography in schools and libraries. The following are excerpts from ACLU Policy 4, with emphasis added (see appendix I).

(a) "The ACLU opposes *any* restraint on the right to create, publish or distribute materials to adults . . . on the basis of obscenity . . ."

(b) "Laws which punish the distribution or exposure of such materials [i.e. including obscenity] to *minors* violate the First Amendment . . ."

(d) "The ACLU believes that . . . *all* limitations of expression on the ground of obscenity . . . are unconstitutional."

(g) "The ACLU opposes on First Amendment grounds laws that restrict the production and distribution of any . . . materials *even when some of the producers of those materials are punishable under criminal law.*" [This describes child pornography.]

The ACLU position on filtering is consistent with their above mentioned policy:

> If adults are allowed full access, but minors are forced to use blocking programs, constitutional problems remain. Minors, especially older minors, have a constitutional right to access many of the resources that have been shown to be blocked by user-based blocking programs. . . . Library blocking proposals that allow minors full access to the Internet only with parental permission are unacceptable.[20]

The ACLU is currently waging a campaign to block filtering. They are threatening expensive lawsuits against public libraries that install Internet filtering software. Sadly we are beginning to see confirmed instances of the ACLU's expensive lawsuits against libraries.

In my opinion, the choice to install Internet filtering software should be left to the individual library, its board, and its patrons. If the library chooses to implement such software to protect children from online pornography and other risks, then these institutions should not have to endure the intimidation and expense of lawsuits by the ACLU.

When children hooked up to the Internet in libraries in Loudoun County, Virginia, they were protected from online pornography through filtering software. The Loudoun County Library Board had voted to ensure that children and other library patrons accessed a family-friendly Internet. (See Model Policy on Internet Sexual Harassment in appendix G.) But in a cyberlaw first, the national ACLU, the ACLU of Virginia, and People for the American Way, on behalf of a diverse group of plaintiffs, are seeking to intervene with a lawsuit over the use of Internet filters in Loudoun County libraries. The

ACLU's complaint charges that the library board is "removing books from the shelves" of the Internet with value to both adults and minors in violation of the Constitution.

Lawyers defending the Loudoun County libraries' right to implement software on library computers with Internet access state, "We accept that the Internet is entitled to robust judicial protection, both for publishers and readers. That protection does not, however, lead to a constitutional right of access through a public facility." They state further, "In essence they [the plaintiffs] claim a constitutional right to have publicly financed peep shows in the Loudoun Library. To state such a claim is to refute it. The First Amendment guarantees no such right."[21]

Jean Armour Polly, Net-mom and former librarian, recently became the spokesperson for GuardiaNet, a server-based filtering software. Polly, along with others, is working to meet the objections of the ALA's staunchest advocates for unrestricted Internet access by offering tools that help to meet some of these arguments.

Evaluating Software Solutions for Schools and Libraries

The Web site "Filtering Facts" was created by a librarian to help parents, educators, and librarians evaluate software solutions appropriate for schools and libraries:

Filtering Facts

http://www.filteringfacts.org
Extensive archive of library-filtering-controversy press coverage, links to pro- and antifiltering sites, and list of filtering solutions that meet or exceed Filtering Facts' criteria.

Choosing Solutions

Some schools and libraries have already established solid Internet use policies and implemented software solutions that will either reduce student exposure to on-line risks or eliminate risks altogether by implementing closed solutions. Server-based blocking/filtering solutions work very well in schools since these software solutions can be implemented at the school's server and will have applications to all computers connected to that server. End-user software is also an option; however, it could become burdensome to install it on each of the five hundred or so computers in a large school. As highlighted in chapter 6, many of the server-based solutions offer great flexibility and customizability for the school administration and/or teachers. Some place the content selection process in the hands of teachers, librarians, or administrators who can modify a blocked list or an allowable list. Software customizability is helping to alleviate censorship objections.

In fact certain server-based solutions allow each computer to be individually configured for classroom and teacher. Most software can be turned off with an adult password that allows teachers enormous flexibility in the classroom. Again, none of the blocking/filtering software is 100 percent effective with respect to blocking inappropriate content. This is where a good acceptable-use policy, student education, and school rules are extremely important.

Some schools are opting for closed systems. Because the Internet is so vast and desired classroom information and research are often so specific, closed software solutions designed specifically for schools, such as EdView, provide two major benefits: (1) 100 percent student safety online, and (2) teacher-approved Web sites that have been prescreened and categorized by academic level.

School Software Solutions

I predict more and more software solutions will emerge to meet the needs of schools. Here is a partial list of software solutions designed specifically for the school market:

Bascom's AME

EdView

GuardiaNet

I Gear

NetFilter (SafeSurf, Kidznet, RCNET)

Scholastic Network

Smart Filter

WatchGuard Schoolmate

X-Stop

Cyber Patrol and SurfWatch server-based products are also being utilized by schools.

The Effectiveness of Software Solutions

At a hearing on Internet Indecency, Elizabeth Whitaker from Tucson Unified School District in Tucson, Arizona, stated that her school district has a three-pronged approach to dealing with inappropriate materials on the Internet. First, they make the students responsible for their actions and hold them to the guidelines and consequences in their Student Rights and Responsibilities handbook. Second, they emphasize that teachers must monitor students using the Internet. Third, they have a technical support that filters out identified unacceptable sites. They assure everyone that the technical filter is no guarantee that unacceptable material will not be accessed, and on occasion a few students have successfully gained unrestricted Internet access. However, in the long run, says Whitaker, filtering has made the use of the Internet easier for her schools.[22]

Get Involved

The home/school connection is our opportunity as parents to become more involved in our children's education in all areas, not just with regard to Internet access. If we can connect our computers with the school network, we will be able to keep up with school announcements and communicate with our children's teachers. We can also use e-mail to leave messages with other parents or teachers about the school and our children's activities.

In the School

As you begin to get involved in your child's classroom online, you will not be alone. Many telephone and cable companies have announced major initiatives to provide Internet connections to schools. Computer hardware and software companies are also donating significant amounts of equipment to schools. And many states and cities, professional associations, and civic groups are getting involved.

Take a look at the following ways you can get involved with and support the use of technology at your child's school:

- Help your child's school obtain used equipment from government agencies or businesses. For information on computer recycling, visit http://www.microweb .com/pepsite/Recycle/recycle_index.html.

- Help your school and community participate in NetDay, a grassroots volunteer effort to wire schools so their computers are networked and have Internet access, at http://www.netday.org.
- Share your expertise by volunteering in your child's classroom or computer lab.
- Organize a training session for teachers and other parents.
- Ask your local PTA to set up a "family night" on computers, technology, and the Internet.
- Help your child's school develop "rules of the road" for students who go online.
- Join the school's technology planning group.
- Ask a teacher if you can observe or join in with your child on the computer.
- Ask the principal to set up a meeting to talk with parents about the school's goals concerning technology.
- Find out whether your school has a technology plan. If so, become familiar with it. If not, identify which teachers are most interested and encourage them to develop a plan.[23]
- Insist that the school implement a responsible Internet use policy *and* software solutions to ensure that students' Internet access is safe and educational.
- Check out the America Links Up campaign materials for Kids Online Week at http://www.amer icalinksup.org.

Seven Questions to Ask Your Librarian

Find out where your library stands on Internet access by asking your librarian the following questions:

1. Do you have computers with Internet access available for patron use?
2. Does the library use a closed Internet system or is filtering or blocking software provided for terminals accessible to minor children? If so, what product is used?
3. Do you have an Internet use policy? If so, may I have a copy?
4. If no policy is in place, how do you deal with patrons who access illegal material on library computers?
5. Is there a time limit placed on patrons using computers?
6. Do you provide training for children and parents with respect to safe Internet access?
7. If no Internet use policy and/or software technology is in place to protect children from online risk of exposure to pornography or predators, are you open to considering such measures?[24]

If your library is providing unrestricted access to the Internet, they are providing a way for children and adults to access illegal material. Find out who holds final responsibility for library policies (start with the library board of directors or trustees) and contact them about implementing an effective Internet use policy that includes the use of software tools for your library. For more information about software solutions for libraries, see appendix C.

Whatever your circumstances, if you want to reduce children's risks online, I recommend that you engage other parents, teachers, school administrators, and librarians of your community in discussions on the need to implement software solutions and Internet use policies and the importance of teacher/librarian or other adult supervision.

As parents, educators, librarians, and child advocates, we must develop an awareness of what is needed and what actions we should take to ensure that our children have what they need for a safe, educational, and entertaining experience on the Internet. While I believe that curriculum and the scope of legal materials accessible at the school and library should be left to the discretion of those individuals and/or boards charged with the duty of selection, I would also suggest that an Internet use policy and technology plan, which includes appropriate software solutions, be implemented. Both are essential to limit children's access to pornographic material and to reduce exposure to online predators. Schools and libraries *do* have the right *and* the obligation to limit the materials they make available to the public, particularly children.

I strongly believe both schools and libraries must take reasonable steps to ensure that the online experiences of all children are safe and educational.

Internet School Filtering Act of 1998 (S.1619 and HR.3177)

This act, which would require schools and libraries receiving federal funds via universal service assistance to block pornographic content by selecting and implementing the filtering technology that best suits their community standards, is before Congress as of June 1998. The bill specifically excludes any U.S. government involvement in determining which content is inappropriate for minors. If passed, the law would require that minor children's Internet access be restricted on all school computers and on at least one computer in libraries. However, parents should still be actively involved in the school and library's development and implementation of their Internet use policies, including the choice of filtering solutions and the type of content to be filtered.

If the bill is passed and signed into law by President Clinton, it then must withstand any lawsuits, which may be filed against it by such organizations as the ACLU.

Cybersavvy Quiz #6

Take the following quiz to see how cybersavvy you are. Then review this chapter and use the glossary to get more specific information on areas that are confusing or unclear.

Choose as many answers as apply.

1. Children access the Internet most often:
   a. in their bedrooms
   b. away from home
   c. in their sleep
   d. on their own computers
2. The educational benefits for schools with access to the Internet include:
   a. ways to enter the Nobel Prize competitions
   b. direct access to experts
   c. computer war games
   d. video conferencing
3. The strategies for safe Internet access at school and the library include:
   a. baby-sitters
   b. software solutions
   c. restrictions that put time limits on hacking
   d. Internet acceptable-use policies
4. Some questions you should ask your librarian include:
   a. What time does the library close?
   b. Does the library implement software solutions to protect kids from pornography on the Internet?
   c. Do you have the book *Kids Online*?
   d. Do you have an Internet use policy?
5. Some ways that you can get involved with and support the use of technology at your child's school include:

a. helping to plan the senior prom
b. sharing your expertise by volunteering in your child's classroom or computer lab
c. sending "cookies" to the computer class
d. helping your child's school develop "rules of the road" for students who go online

Scoring: If you chose the letters B and D for every question, you answered correctly. Congratulations! If you missed several answers, take some time to reread this chapter.

For further information on protecting children at school or the library, refer to the following resources and see appendixes A, C, and G.

Library Action Manual, Enough Is Enough

A Practical Guide to Internet Filters, Karen G. Schneider

How can I help shape the safety issues
of the Internet?

What does family-friendly policy look like?

What roles do industry leaders and the
law enforcement community have
in Internet safety?

8

It Takes All of Us

"Tom, would you take a look at this letter?" asked Susan. "I just want to support those who are sticking their necks out to support our requests."

"Yeah, with all these lawsuits, I guess it is risky," Tom said as he put down the TV remote control. "I fully support First Amendment rights, but not at Lily's expense. She has rights, too! Besides, illegal content and activity are not constitutionally protected." Tom turned his attention to Susan's letter.

Dear Board Member,

Congratulations for taking a courageous stand in favor
of protecting the children of this city! You and the entire

185

library board are to be commended for taking proactive measures to provide safe travel on the Internet to all library patrons through your Internet use policy.

I am relieved to discover that the policy states that e-mail, chat rooms, newsgroups, and all areas that harbor potential risks to children and adults will not be available. I am also glad to hear that the library will install blocking software to protect children from accessing illegal material.

Nevertheless, I realize that filtering and blocking cannot be relied on to be 100 percent effective, so I appreciate that the library staff has strategically located the computers with Internet access so that they will be able to monitor their use.

I recognize that, as a parent, I must still be diligent in supervising my child; however, the library board, in its responsible attitude toward upholding community standards, has made my job of parenting a little bit easier and a lot less worrisome. Thank you!

"Good letter, Susan!" Tom said with pride. "You just forgot to sign it."

How can the Internet become safe for my child, my family, and future generations?

The answer lies in a shared responsibility among the public (parents, educators, librarians, and others who supervise children), the high-tech industry, and law enforcement. Each provides a layer of protection and security for the safety of kids online. And whenever one of these entities endeavors to accept its responsibility for child safety online, we need to affirm and support those efforts.

Why is it important to become involved in making the Internet safe for children? The answer is two-dimensional. First, the Internet is an invaluable resource that can benefit children. It is an incredible source of education and information to which every child needs access. The second reason to be involved is the vast potential for pollution of the Internet, which destroys its value to everyone. Even if you take measures to completely prevent unacceptable material from invading your home, your child will certainly be impacted by others who are exposed to Internet pornography such as other kids, baby-sitters, or relatives. The secondhand effects of pornography can be devastating, just as the secondhand effects of cigarette smoke are. In my opinion it's only a matter of time before the effects of proliferating pornography on the Internet produce a coarsening of attitudes toward women and children, lessening their dignity and value in our culture.

Let's not let a medium that has such value be polluted by illegal pornography and sexual predators and, in essence, taken away from our children.

In the last few chapters, I have focused on what parents and child advocates can do to ensure that our children have a safe, educational, and entertaining experience while exploring the new frontiers of cyberspace at home, in school, and at the library. In this last chapter, I want to help you understand how you can make a difference—how you can help shape the safety of this medium as it develops.

Public Awareness

Some people don't understand the Internet or are intimidated by it. Many don't understand the risks involved in Internet access and the available solutions to guard against those risks. Still others haven't bought into this vast new world, because they haven't recognized the enormous benefits it offers. All combined, public awareness programs for parents, educators, librarians, and community caregivers who supervise children are essential since these people are the ones most involved in making decisions to keep the Internet safe. Public awareness programs need to include the following:

- a description of the benefits and risks online
- training for surfing the Net and using technological tools
- safety tips for online use
- information on how to get involved with the online policies and technological solutions at schools and public libraries
- a strategy for encouraging the technology industry to continue developing and implementing software solutions
- a challenge to demand more aggressive enforcement of existing laws

I have tried to design this book so that it can be used not only as a public awareness tool but as a training manual and a "take action" plan for parents and others involved in the supervision of children. As I've stressed before, parents are the first line of defense for protecting their own children on the Internet. Simply by reading this book, you are increasing your awareness of the issues surrounding child safety online and thereby becoming better equipped to ensure that your child's online experience is safe, educational, and entertaining.

You'll find additional resources in the appendices for your further education and guidance. This book is just a first course. Because the Internet and surrounding technologies are growing and changing every day, it is important for you to keep up to speed. I hope you will use these resources to further your awareness. By accessing the information in the resource lists and other appendices that give Web sites, you will be able to get the most up-to-date information regarding child safety and other issues. This is the beauty of the Internet—current information at your fingertips, with a simple click of the mouse, twenty-four hours a day.

America Links Up: Kids Online Week (September 1998)

America Links Up is a public awareness campaign designed to help parents, educators, and all community caregivers learn the medium of the Internet, understand online issues, and learn how to use existing software tools that can help enrich children's online experiences. The America Links Up Campaign was created in response to the critical need for a public awareness and education campaign recognized by industry, nonprofit, and government participants in the 1997 Internet Online Summit: Focus on Children. The Summit (planned by America Online, American Library Association, AT&T, Center for Democracy & Technology, Center for Media Education, Children Now, Children's Partnership, Education Development Center, Enough Is Enough, Microsoft, National Association of Secondary School Principals, National Center for Missing & Exploited Children, National Consumers League, National Education Association, National Law Center, National Education Network, the Walt Disney Company, and Time Warner) was organized to find solutions to safety concerns created by the Internet. To learn more about America Links Up, visit http://www.americalinksup.org.

Technology Industry

While it is helpful for us to understand what we can
do to protect our children, the burden of protecting children from pornography flowing into our homes, schools,
and libraries does not rest entirely with parents and
those who supervise children. There are at least three
areas where the technology industry needs to bear the
burden for safety on the Internet:

- Industry leaders must increasingly adopt family-
  friendly corporate policy.
- Industry leaders need to implement technological
  solutions at the server level, such as filtered services
  or parental controls.
- Industry leaders must comply with existing laws.

The new technologies being developed will allow
providers to offer their wares to selected audiences, supply more reliable ways of screening out unwanted customers, and revoke subscription privileges of customers
who don't abide by provider policies.

You may be thinking, *So what's my role?* Remember,
the Internet industry is a business. Market demand
drives business, and as there is increasing demand for
safe and clean Internet access, the Internet industry will
respond by supplying safe solutions.

You can also play a vital and important role by hold-
ing your Internet service provider or online service
provider accountable to their commitment to family-
friendly corporate policy. And if your existing ISP or
OSP does not have family-friendly policies, you may
want to take your business elsewhere. What constitutes
family-friendly policy? The following is a partial list:

- Provision of either server-based filtered service, end-user software solutions (preferably free of charge to subscribers), or parental controls.
- Compliance with existing cyberporn laws (i.e., removal of illegal pornography, child pornography, and obscenity from their own proprietary service and USENET newsgroups that offer such material).
- Segregation of adult content from children or no access to adult content. This type of policy conveys an additional layer of corporate commitment to families.
- Response in a timely fashion to your concerns and complaints.
- Cooperation with law enforcement in working toward a safe Internet.

As Enough Is Enough's representative on the steering committee for the 1997 Internet Online Summit: Focus on Children, I developed a comprehensive ISP pledge to children, which was later condensed to the following proposed ethics code. This was submitted to the ISP/Law Enforcement Committee working on the Summit. Though it was not adopted, due to the many complex issues surrounding vast sign-off by national associations representing the ISP community, the goal of family-friendly corporate policy regarding online safety is continuing to be encouraged at the national level.

Suggested Code of Ethical Conduct for ISPs and OSPs

1. We will adopt terms-of-service policies:
   - forbidding the use of our service to post child pornography or hard-core pornography, or to

make sexual or other improper solicitation of
children;

- stating that we will promptly address violations of these policies;
- stating that we reserve the right to take action
  in good faith to restrict availability of material
  that we consider to be obscene, lewd, lascivious, filthy, excessively violent, harassing, or
  otherwise objectionable, whether or not such
  material is constitutionally protected.

2. We will remove illegal material hosted on our own
   system when advised of its presence.
3. We will not subscribe to newsgroups (or bulletin
   boards or other forums) in which illegal activity
   occurs, including the posting of child pornography or hard-core pornography or sexual or other
   improper solicitations to children.
4. We will enable or offer server-level filtering of illegal material
   OR
   We will offer parental controls as the default setting for access by a minor under age seventeen,
   which default can be disabled by the master account holder.
5. We will cooperate with local, state, federal, and international authorities in the investigation of
   crimes involving use of our service, to the extent
   practical and lawful, including the retention of
   user information and evidence for a reasonable
   time and the reporting of any suspected incidents
   of child abuse to the proper authorities.[1]

At that same summit, Vice President Al Gore challenged the online industry to come up with ways to protect children's privacy, shield them from exploitative

marketing, and provide them with more safe places to go online. "Industry will never be able to meet [the need of America's families]," said Gore, "unless it devotes the same resources and commitment to designing parental controls that it would devote to the design and launch of any new product." Gore went on to announce that the leading Internet Service Provider Associations had made a new agreement to cooperate with law enforcement authorities on a zero-tolerance policy against child pornography. The zero-tolerance policy against child pornography emerged from this suggested code of ethical conduct. It's not everything I had envisioned, but it's a great start! Once again, you can make a difference by making sure that your ISP/OSP is adhering to the zero-tolerance policy and by encouraging your provider to adopt this or a similar code of ethical conduct in an effort to exercise corporate responsibility.

Law Enforcement/Law Makers

U.S. law enforcement has recently made protecting children in cyberspace a priority. The FBI has increased its staff related to combating computer-related exploitation of children by 50 percent in the past six months, and has established a task force that specializes in computer child pornography and solicitation cases. In addition, the Attorney General's Advisory Committee is providing training and information about the latest computer technology for law enforcement and prosecutors across the country.

Still, with the lack of enforcement of obscenity laws, it seems that the perpetrators, producers, and distributors of pornography (the individuals profiting the most) are the only ones who have not been required to bear any responsibility or accountability under the law.

In print and broadcast where pornography laws have been more aggressively prosecuted, pornographers bear some burden of responsibility. For example, we rarely receive child pornography in the mailbox, and it's difficult to find in adult bookstores. But in cyberspace, this is not true. Even a few prosecutions could greatly discourage the Internet distribution of child pornography and obscenity.

Imagine a community that allows corporations to dump toxic waste into the air and water supply. Either the community has no laws regarding this behavior, or the existing laws are not being enforced. Real communities enforce standards of behavior. They expect their members to act responsibly.

By supporting more aggressive enforcement of cybercrime laws, you can help build those standards of responsibility. Remember, public opinion drives public policy and law enforcement! Here again, you can make a difference by demanding that existing laws are prosecuted and enforced. Many of those making the decisions of law enforcement priority are elected officials—your voice and your vote have power.

You can make a difference by letting your local, state, and federal legislators and officials know that you consider these needs a priority. Law enforcement can be greatly empowered to enforce existing laws with the necessary financial resources, technology tools, and training. This is true not only at the local level, but at the state and national levels as well.

The areas where the law enforcement community needs to share the burden for children's safety on the Internet include:

- aggressive enforcement of existing cyberporn and child stalking laws

- the provision of education, tools, training, and resources that law enforcers need to do their jobs
- local law enforcement computer training specific to investigating and prosecuting cybercrimes
- creating new laws and/or updating existing laws to extend protection of kids in cyberspace

Congressional Internet Caucus

The public is invited to visit the new Internet Caucus Advisory Committee Web site at http://www.netcaucus.org. You will find the latest information on the programs and initiatives of the bipartisan Congressional Internet Caucus, made up of more than one hundred representatives from both the House and Senate. In addition, you'll find comprehensive resources on Internet-related issues before Congress. Even though you can't e-mail individual members of Congress at the site, most members of Congress have Web sites and e-mail so that they can hear from their constituents on the issues that concern them.

Why It Will Take All of Us

You *can* make a difference. Here are stories of what others have done.

First, she changed her family's phone number; then, she changed their address along with her daughter's school. Deborah Boehle says that her nine-year-old daughter "was robbed of her childhood" as a result of an Internet prank that caused the girl's name and number along with sexually explicit messages to be posted systemwide. Boehle went public with her daughter's case after becoming exasperated at learning that the illegal Internet posting, if investigated and prosecuted under state law, is treated as a low-grade misdemeanor.

Boehle says her daughter's name, phone number, and address began appearing on at least fourteen Internet listings along with lewd messages. Boehle is working with Republican Congressman from Illinois Jerry Well, local police, and prosecutors in drafting legislation that would make this type of incident a criminal offense that carries a harsh penalty. The legislation would make it illegal to use the Internet to target an individual under age sixteen for sexually explicit messages or contacts. Convictions under the proposed law would be classified as felonies punishable with fines or by imprisonment of up to five years. An initiative is under way in Illinois to attack harassment and exploitation of minors through electronic communications in the form of an Internet criminal activity unit.[2]

Hannah Wheeler (not her real name) called the Enough Is Enough office one day and shared her family's story. Her two daughters, six and eight years old, attended a birthday party at the home of Ronald Riva. Her daughters later shared with her that Mr. Riva had molested them.

Hannah contacted the police, which led to the investigation, indictment, and conviction of Riva and his conspirator, Melton Myers. Both men were sentenced to life in prison without parole. In addition, sixteen members of a child pornography production ring (the Orchid Club, mentioned in chapter 3) were indicted. In one instance, Riva and Myers coerced a ten-year-old girl to pose in sexually explicit positions in real time over the Internet for their own sexual gratification and that of other members of the Orchid Club.

Because Hannah and her daughters were courageous enough to cooperate with authorities, these men can no longer harm children!

Why is it so important that we collectively deal with the proliferation of pornography on the Internet, especially that which is illegal, as well as the abundance of pedophile activity in this new communications medium?

First, for the Internet to survive as well as fulfill its potential as the communications vehicle of the future, it must achieve mainstream acceptance. As one of the most important developments in the history of communications, the Internet must become a safe *and* worthwhile medium for all users.

Second, with converging technologies, we need to move forward on Internet safety issues before the majority of American households, schools, and libraries have Internet access bundled with their telephone and cable TV systems. Imagine how complicated it will be to protect children from viewing hard-core pornography on their family-room TV.

Historically, it has been shown that the pornography in sexually oriented businesses, such as adult bookstores and strip clubs, has a harmful effect on the surrounding communities. "The best professional judgment available indicates overwhelmingly that adult entertainment businesses—even a relatively passive use such as an adult bookstore—have serious negative effect on their immediate environs."[3] Some of the negative effects on the community include higher incidences of sex-related crimes as well as violent crimes, such as homicide, rape, and assault. In addition, many communities have experienced a loss of property values when sexually oriented businesses moved in.

What does all this have to do with pornography on the Internet? No longer do people have to go to the seedy side of town to visit adult bookstores, peep shows, and strip clubs. No longer do collectors of bestiality have to search for this material on the black market. No longer do pedophiles have to go underground to distribute and access illegal child pornography. They can access it in the privacy of their own homes. If pornography outlets and other sexually oriented businesses have historically had a negative impact on their surrounding communities, how much more will be the negative effects on our children as pornography permeates our culture via the Internet? The seedy side of town has come to them!

Why should you and I get involved to help make the Internet safe? Because we are our children's first line of defense, and now is the time to have an influence in the development of the Internet. The Internet's explosion into the majority of homes, schools, libraries, and offices in this country is bound to be felt around the world. There are many issues that confront this new medium. I want to challenge you to work alongside those of us at the grass roots as well as at the national and international levels, who are seeking solutions that will ensure a safe and secure Internet that will truly reach its wonderful potential.

While you may continue to feel overwhelmed or intimidated by the Internet pitfalls presented in this book, remember that you do not have to shoulder the burden of online safety by yourself. Protecting our children on the Internet is a shared responsibility! Take advantage of the resources you find in these pages. You are not powerless, and you are not alone!

Appendix A
Resources for Kids and Parents

Web Sites, Books, Pamphlets, Videos, and Organizations

Web Sites

Good Content Sites for Kids

Berit's Best Sites for Children
http://db.cochran.com/li_toc:
theoPage.dh

Children's Express
http://www.ce.org

Children's Television Workshop
http://www.ctw.org

Cuisenaire Learning Place
http://www.cuisenaire.com

The Dinosaur Society
http://www.dinosociety.org

Disney Daily Blast
http://www.disneyblast.com

The Exploratorium
http://www.exploratorium.edu

Family Internet
http://www.familyinternet.com

Franklin Institute Science Museum
http://sln.fi.edu/

Freezone
http://www.freezone.com

Globalearn
http://www.globalearn.org

Internet Family Fun
http://www.worldvillage.com/family
fun/sites.htm

Internet Public Library Youth Division
http://www.ipl.org/youth

Internet Weather
http://cfa165.harvard.edu/weather
.html

JASON Project
http://www.jasonproject.org

Jean Armour Polly's Internet Kids & Family Yellow Pages
http://www.well.com/user/polly/ikyp

Job Smart: Career Guides
http://www.jobsmart.org/tools/career

KidsCom
http://www.kidscom.com

Kids' Korner
http://www.kids-korner.com

Library of Congress
http://www.loc.gov

The Metropolitan Museum of Art
http://www.metmuseum.org/htmlfile/education/kid.html

NASA
http://spacelink.msfc.nasa.gov

Nickelodeon Online
http://www.nick.com

PBS Online
http://www.pbs.org

Steve Savitzhky's Interesting Places for Kids
http://www.starport.com/places/forkids

Supersite for Kids
http://www.bonus.com

Teen Guide to Making Money
http://www.tfs.net/personal/ gbyron

Time Warner Inc.
http://www.pathfinder.com
http://www.parenttime.com
http://www.kids.warnerbros.com
http://cartoonnetwork.com

Time Warner Sports Illustrated for Kids Online
http://www.sikids.com

Warner Bros. Online
http://www.warnerbros.com

The White House
http://www.whitehouse.gov

The White House for Kids
http://www.whitehouse.gov/WH/kids/html/kidshome.html

Sites to Help Parents Protect Kids

The Child Abuse Yellow Pages
http://idealist.com/cayp

Child Quest International
http://www.childquest.org

Congressional Internet Caucus
http://www.netcaucus.org

Cyberangels
http://www.cyberangels.org

Enough Is Enough
http://www.enough.org

Family Education Network
http://familyeducation.com

Family PC
http://www.familypc.com

Filtering Facts
http://www.filteringfacts.org

Focus on the Family
http://www.family.org/cforum

Internet Online Summit: America Links Up Campaign
http://www.kidsonline.org

Kidshield
http://www.kidshield.com

Kids Online
http://www.protectkids.com

LegalPad and Legal-Pad Jr (for Kids)
http://www.legalpad.com

Moms Club/Moms Online
http://www.momsonline.com

The National Crime Prevention Council Presents McGruff & Scruff and the Crime Dogs
http://www.crimedog.com
800-WE PREVENT

National Parent Information Network
http://ericps.ed.uiuc/edu/npin
800-583-4135

Parent Soup
http://www.parentsoup.com

PICS
http://www.w3.org/PICS

Safeguarding Our Children— United Mothers (SOC-UM)
http://www.soc-um.org

SafeSurf
http://www.safesurf.com

The Sage Letter
http://www.sageway.com

Web Emergency—Child Alert Network
A Division of SOC-UM
http://www.we-can.org

Web Wise Kids
http://www.webwisekids.com

Additional Resources

Print

Aftab, Parry. *A Parent's Guide to the Internet.* New York: SC Press, 1997.

Anderson, Neil. *Bondage Breaker.* Eugene, Oreg.: Harvest House, 1993.

Baehr, Ted. *The Media-Wise Family.* Colorado Springs: Chariot/Victor Publishing, 1998.

Baker, Jason D. *Christian Cyberspace Companion: A Guide to the Internet and Christian Online Resources.* 2d ed. Grand Rapids: Baker Books, 1997.

Britton, Zachary. *SafetyNet: Guiding and Guarding Your Children on the Internet.* Eugene, Oreg.: Harvest House, 1998.

Brooks, Gary. *Centerfold Syndrome: How Men Can Overcome Objectification and Achieve Intimacy with Women.* Jossey-Bass, 1996.

Bruno, Bonnie, and Joel Comm. *Internet Family Fun: The Parent's Guide to Safe Surfing.* San Francisco: No Starch Press, 1997. 800-788-3123.

Colson, Charles. *Pornography: A Human Tragedy.* Wheaton: Tyndale House, 1986.

Cranor, Lorrie Faith, and Paul Resnick. *Internet Online Summit Technology Inventory,* November 24, 1997, available at http://www.research.att.com/projects/tech4kids.

Dinsmore, M. and W. *Homeschool Guide to the Internet.* P.O. Box 254, Elkton, MD 21922-0254: Homeschool Press, 1996.

Falk, B. *The Internet Roadmap*. Sybex, 1994. 800-227-2346.

Ferguson, Donna. *The Assault on America's Children*. Newport Beach, Calif.: Harbor House West, 1994.

———. *The Someday Kid*. Newport Beach, Calif.: Harbor House West, 1993.

Hall, Laurie. *An Affair of the Mind*. Colorado Springs: Focus on the Family, 1996.

Hattemer, Barbara, and Rob Showers. *Don't Touch That Dial*. Lafayette, La.: Hunting House, 1993.

Hoffman, P. E. *Internet Instant Reference*. Sybex, 1994. 800-227-2346.

Kavanagh, Stephen J. *Protecting Children in Cyberspace*. Springfield, Va.: Behavioral Psychotherapy Center, 1997.

Marsh, M. *Everything You Need to Know (But Were Afraid to Ask Kids) about the Information Superhighway*. P.O. Box 60967, Palo Alto, Calif. 60967: Computer Learning Foundation, 1995.

Murphy, J. and K. Tucker. *Stay Tuned! Raising Media-Savvy Kids in the Age of the Channel-Surfing Couch Potato*. New York: Doubleday, 1996.

Payne, Leanne. *The Broken Image*. Grand Rapids: Baker Books, 1996.

Perkins, M., and C. Nunez. *Kidware: The Parent's Guide to Software for Children*. Prima Publishing, 1994.

Polly, Jean Armour (Net-mom). *The Internet Kids and Family Yellow Pages*. Berkeley, Calif.: Osborne/McGraw-Hill, 1997. More information about the author is available at her home page: http://www.netmom.com.

Reisman, Judith A. *Kinsey: Crimes and Consequences*. Arlington, Va.: The Institute for Media Education (P.O. Box 7404, Arlington, VA 22207), 1998.

Schneider, Karen G. *A Practical Guide to Internet Filters*. New York: Neal-Schuman, 1997.

Turkle, S. *Life on the Screen: Identity in the Age of the Internet*. New York: Simon & Schuster, 1995.

Videos

CyberSafe
Parallel Productions, Inc.
7486 Hardisty St.
West Bloomfield, MI 48324
248-363-1442

Empty Embrace
Enough Is Enough
P.O. Box 888
Fairfax, VA 22030
888-2-ENOUGH

Organizations and Government Agencies

American Academy of Pediatrics
601 13th Street NW, Suite 400
North
Washington, DC 20005
800-433-9016
http://www.aap.org

American Center for Law and Justice
P.O. Box 64429
Virginia Beach, VA 23467
757-226-2489
http://www.aclj.org

American Family Association
P.O. Drawer 2440
Tupelo, MS 38803
800-326-4543
http://www.afa.net

American Library Association
50 E. Huron Street
Chicago, IL 60611
312-280-5044
http://www.ala.org

Center for Children and Technology
96 Morton Street, 7th Floor
New York, NY 10014
212-807-4200
http://www.edc.org/CCT

Center for Democracy and Technology
1634 Eye Street NW, Suite 1100
Washington, DC 20006
202-637-9800
http://www.cdt.org

Center for Media Education
1511 K Street NW, Suite 518
Washington, DC 20005
202-628-2620
Publications:
Web of Deception: Threats to Children from Online Marketing
http://www.cme.org

Child Lures
5166 Shelburne Road
Shelburne, VT 05482
802-985-8458
Publications:
Child Lures Family Guide for Prevention of Sexual Abuse and Abduction
Child Lures School Program for Prevention of Sexual Abuse and Abduction
http://www.childlures.com

Childnet International
317 South Division #198
Ann Arbor, MI 48104
313 572-4595
http://www.childnet-int.org

Child Quest International, Inc.
1625 The Alameda
Suite 400
San Jose, CA 95126
408-287-4673
http://www.childquest.org

Children Now
1212 Broadway, Suite 530
Oakland, CA 94612
510-763-2444
http://www.childrennow.org

Children's Defense Fund
25 E Street NW
Washington, DC 20001
202-628-8787
http://www.childrensdefense.org

The Children's Partnership
1351 3rd Street Promenade, Suite 206
Santa Monica, CA 90401
310-260-1220

Publications:
America's Children and the
Information Superhighway
The Parents' Guide to the
Information Superhighway
http://www.childrenspartnership.org

Concerned Women for America
370 L'Enfant Promenade SW
Suite 800
Washington, DC 20024
202-488-7000
http://www.cwfa.org

Consumer Federation of America
1424 16th Street NW, Suite 604
Washington, DC 20036
202-387-6121

Consumers Union
1666 Connecticut Avenue NW,
Suite 310
Washington, DC 20009
202-462-6262
http://www.consunion.org

CyberSmart
201 Lloyd Road
Bernardsville, NJ 07924
908-221-1516

Direct Marketing Association
1120 Avenue of the Americas
New York, NY 10036-6700
212-768-7277
Publication:
Get CyberSavvy
http://www.the-dma.org

ECPAT—USA
End Child Prostitution, Child
Pornography and Trafficking of
Children for Sexual Purposes
475 Riverside Drive
New York, NY 10115
212-870-2427

Education Development Center
Children's Safety Network
National Network of Violence
Prevention Practitioners
Center For Violence and Injury
Prevention
55 Chapel Street
Newton, MA 02158-1060
617-969-7100
http://www.edc.org

The Elijah Initiative
P.O. Box 242
Cambridge, VT 05444
http://www.edc.org

Enough Is Enough
P.O. Box 888
Fairfax, VA 22030
888-2-ENOUGH or 714-435-9056
Publications:
Bibliography
The Internet Safety Kit
Library Action Manual
The Take Action Manual: What
One Woman Can Do
http://www.enough.org

Family Friendly Libraries
President, Karen Jo Gounaud
http://www.fflibraries.org
e-mail: ffl@compuserve.com

Family Research Council
801 G Street NW
Washington, DC 20001
202-393-2100
http://www.frc.org

Focus on the Family
8605 Explorer Drive
Colorado Springs, CO 80920
800-A-Family
http://www.family.org

Highlights for Children
803 Church Street
Honesdale, PA 18431
800-255-9517

KidsNet
6856 Eastern Avenue NW, Suite 208
Washington, DC 20012
202-291-1400
e-mail: kidsnet@aol.com

Kids Safe
17939 Chatsworth Street, Suite 525
Granada Hills, CA 91344
800-320-9910
http://www.kidssafe.org

**National Association
of Elementary School Principals**
1615 Duke Street
Alexandria, VA 22314
703-684-3345
http://www.naesp.org

**National Association of
Secondary School Principals**
1904 Association Drive
Reston, VA 20191
703-860-0200
http://www.nassp.org

**National Center for Missing
and Exploited Children**
2101 Wilson Blvd., Suite 550
Arlington, VA 22201-3077
703-235-3900
Publications:
Child Safety on the Information
Highway
Kids and Company: Together for
Safety
Teen Safety on the Information
Highway
http://www.missingkids.com

**National Coalition for the
Protection of Children
and Families**
800 Compton Road, Suite 9224
Cincinnati, OH 45231
513-521-6227
Publication:
Library Protection Package
http://www.nationalcoalition.org

**National Committee to Prevent
Child Abuse**
332 S. Michigan Avenue, Suite 1600
Chicago, IL 60604-4357
312-663-3520
http://www.NCPCA@childabuse.org

National Consumers League
1701 K Street NW, Suite 1201
Washington, DC 20006
202-835-3323
http://www.natlconsumersleague.org

National Education Association
1201 16th Street NW
Washington, DC 20036
202-833-4000
http://www.nea.org

**National Law Center
for the Protection
of Children and Families**
4103 Chain Bridge Road, Suite 410
Fairfax, VA 22030
703-691-4626
http://www.nationallawcenter.org

**National Parent Teacher
Association**
330 Wabash Avenue, Suite 2100
Chicago, IL 60611
312-670-6782
http://www.pta.org

**National School Board
Association**
1680 Duke Street
Alexandria, VA 22314
703-838-6722
http://www.nsba.org

The National Urban League
120 Wall Street

New York, NY 10005
212-558-5300
http://www.nul.org

Plugged In
1923 University Avenue East
Palo Alto, CA 94303
650-322-1134

Project Open
8403 Colesville Road
Silver Spring, MD 20910
301-495-4955
http://www.isa.net/project-open

Strategies for Media Literacy
1095 Market Street #410
San Francisco, CA 94103
415-621-2911

U.S. Department of Education
Office of Educational Research and
   Improvement
555 New Jersey Avenue NW
Washington, DC 20208-5570
800-USA-Learn
Publication:
   Parents Guide to the Internet
http://www.ed.gov

Law Enforcement

U.S. Department of Justice
950 Pennsylvania Avenue NW
Washington, DC 20530
http://www.usdoj.gov

Federal Bureau of Investigation
935 Pennsylvania Avenue NW
Washington, DC 20535-0001

202-324-3000
http://www.fbi.gov

Interpol
200 Quai Charles de Gaulle
69006 Lyon, France
http://www.interpol.com

**International Association
of Chiefs of Police**
515 N. Washington Street
Alexandria, VA 22314-2357
703-836-6767
http://www.theiacp.org

**National Associations
of Chiefs of Police**
3801 Biscayne Blvd.
Miami, FL 33137
305-573-0070
http://www.aphf.org

**National Associations
of Police Organizations**
750 First Street NE, Suite 920
Washington, DC 20002
202-842-4420
http://www.napo.org

United States Attorney General
950 Pennsylvania Avenue NW
Washington, DC 20530-0001
202-514-2000
http://www.usdoj.gov/ag

United States Customs
1300 Pennsylvania Avenue NW
Washington, DC 20229
202-927-1000
http://www.customs.ustreas.gov

Appendix B
Tool Descriptions

The following descriptions are based on those prepared by Lorrie Faith Cranor and Paul Resnick for the *Internet Online Summit Technology Inventory*. (This inventory is updated regularly and can be found at http://www.research.att.com/projects/teach4kids.) I have used the same terminology as is in chapter 6 to explain the functions of the tools: *suggest, search, monitor, inform, warn,* and *block.* Check out the Web sites for further information on specific tools. When you buy a tool it will come with complete instructions on installation. I have not personally evaluated all the software tools discussed in this book. Rather I have relied on information supplied by software manufacturers as the basis for the tool descriptions.

Access Management Engine (AME)
Bascom Global Internet Services, Inc.
http://www.bascom.com
Type of action: Blocks all attempts to access unapproved Internet content; customized to allow or disallow Web sites, USENET news, IRC chat, telnet, gopher, ftp, and all mail
Location: School or ISP

AltaVista Filtered Search Service
Digital Equipment Corporation
http://www.altavista.digital.com
Type of action: Filtered *search* of Web sites based on third-party ratings

Location: Search service sends message back to end-user's computer

America Online Parental Controls
http://www.aol.com
Type of action: Blocks user from accessing all or part of content; includes controls for e-mail, the Web, chat rooms, downloading, and newsgroups; plus Access Only Kid-Approved Sites and Access Only Teen-Approved Sites
Location: ISP as part of the AOL service

Bess
N2H2
http://www.n2h2.com
Type of action: Monitors and *blocks* based on customer's criteria, matched against database of labeled sites
Location: ISP Remote proxy or local proxy

Bonus.com the SuperSite for Kids
(NetScooter, Contour Technology, Desktop Shortcut)
http://www.bonus.com
Type of action: NetScooter acts as a family-friendly *blocking* filter, allowing kids limited access to selected *(suggested)* activities found on the Web
Location: Protected environment on the Web

CleanScreen
CleanScreen Corporation
http://www.cleanscreen.net
Type of action: Blocks, monitors, reports, e-mail and news filtering, site and keyword in context filtering
Location: ISP or proxy server

Click and Browse Jr.
NetWave Inc.
http://www.netwavelink.com
Type of action: Suggest and *block*
Location: End-user's computer

Cyber Patrol
Microsystems
http://www.cyberpatrol.com
Type of action: Internet filter that *blocks* access to content, according to judgments made by supervising adults; shuts down access when it detects tampering; also provides *suggestions* for good sites
Location: End-user's computer, Local Area Networks, and third-party (proxy) servers

CYBERsitter
Solid Oak Software, Inc.
http://www.solidoak.com
Type of action: Monitors Internet activity and *blocks* access to material unsuitable for viewing per PICS rating system
Location: End-user's computer

Cyber Snoop
Pearl Software
http://www.pearlsw.com
Type of action: Monitors, blocks access, and *suggests* sites as defined by administrator
Location: End-user's computer or server

Disney's Daily Blast
http://www.disney.com
Type of action: Blocks by using word filter technology and *suggests;* no browsing capabilities or outbound links to sites except for Disney.com, Family.com, and Advertiser sites; includes Disney's custom D-Mail (control settings) and D-Browser (customized viewing system that restricts access to the Internet)
Location: End-user's computer via D-Browser and SurfWatch

EdView—Secure and Smart Channel to the Internet
http://www.edview.com
Type of action: Suggests; blocks

Location: Available to end-user through EdView server

ESRB
Entertainment Software Rating Board
http://www.esrb.org
Type of action: Labels and *informs* regarding appropriate content on each rated Web site; may *block* rated sites based on preferences
Location: Rating system that displays icons and/or labels used with search engines, browsers, individual Web sites

EvaluWEB
http://www.sserv.com/evaluweb
Type of action: Blocks sites and informs through a banner rating system, which is a graphic
Location: Content ratings service stored at EvaluWEB server

Flash Net
Type of action: Blocks
Location: Clean ISP that utilizes server-based blocking

GuardiaNet
http://www.guardianet.net
Type of action: Monitors by logging access; parents can *block* sites by building filtering lists
Location: End-user's computer accesses control list on GuardiaNet server

IBM Web Traffic Express
http://www.ics.raleigh.ibm.com
Type of action: Blocks
Location: ISP or proxy

I-Gear
http://www.urlabs.com
Type of action: Server-based content management solution for K–12 and libraries; *monitors* and *blocks*
Location: ISP, remote proxy server

IllumaNet
http://www.illuma.net
Type of action: Blocks

Location: ISP and end-user's computer

The Internet Filter, IF Lite, IF Only, IF Researcher
http://www.turnercom.com
Type of action: Blocks; monitors

The Internet Kids & Family Yellow Pages, 2d edition
http://www.netmom.com/
Type of action: Suggests 3,500 Internet resources
Location: Web site and 600-page book

Mayberry USA
http://www.mayberryusa.net
Type of action: Blocks; suggests
Location: clean ISP that utilizes server-based blocking

The Microsoft Network (MSN)
http:www.msn.com
Type of action: If activated, uses the PICS standard with default setting to RSACi ratings; *blocks*.
Location: ISP

NetFilter
http://www.netfilter.com
Type of action: Filtering application that *blocks*, based on key words and database updated automatically every twenty-four hours
Location: ISP

Net Nanny
http://www.netnanny.com
Type of action: Configurable for security, access, and control; *monitors* violations of rules and *blocks* access
Location: End-user's computer and some types of servers

Net-Rated
PC DataPower
http://www.netrated.com
Type of action: Blocks access to identified objectionable sites and *monitors* activities
Location: End-user's computer

**Net Shepherd World Opinion
Rating Service**
Net Shepherd 2.0 client software
http://www.netshepherd.com
http://www.family.netshepherd.com
Type of action: When used with
   PICS-compatible software,
   browser *blocks* access; filtered
   searches allow access only to
   sites with a "general" rating
Location: Server

PlanetView
http://www.planetview.com
Type of action: Filter service that
   blocks
Location: Works with browser

RSACi
http://www.rsac.org
Type of action: PICS-compatible
   content-labeling system that
   works with browser to *block*
Location: End-user's computer
   while using Microsoft Internet
   Explorer

SafeSurf Rating Standard
SafeSurf Internet Filtering
   Solution
http://www.safesurf.com
Type of action: Blocks content based
   on nine adult themes
Location: Server-based Web site,
   local proxy server

Scholastic Network
http://www.scholasticnetwork.com
Type of action: Suggests more than
   four thousand interactive
   projects and activities
Location: Web site

SmartFilter
Secure Computing Corporation
http://www.smartfilter.com

Type of action: Monitors URL access
   and *blocks* undesirable
   categories
Location: Server

SurfWatch
Spyglass, Inc.
http://www.surfwatch.com
Type of action: Blocks access to sites
   based on filtering categories and
   restricts searches
Location: End-user computer,
   LANS, proxy servers, and ISPs

WatchGuard SchoolMate
WatchGuard Technologies, Inc.
http://www.watchguard.com/sm
   .html
Type of action: Blocks access to
   undesirable sites and *monitors*
   visits to real-time graphical
   representations
Location: Stand-alone, dedicated
   network security appliance for
   school network

WebChaperone with iCRT
http://www.webchaperone.com
Type of action:
Location:

WebSENSE
http://www.websense.com
Type of action: Blocks and *monitors*
   traffic to inappropriate Internet
   sites
Location: Server-based

X-Stop
http://www.xstop.com
Type of action: Blocks, warns
Location: End-user computer,
   server

Yahooligans!
http://www.yahooligans.com
Type of action: Search
Location: Search engine

Appendix C
8 Questions about Software Solutions at Libraries

1. How does the Supreme Court decision on the Communications Decency Act (CDA) affect what we do at the local library?

The decision to overturn the indecency provision of the CDA makes providing a closed or filtered Internet system even more imperative, because there is no federal law in place to deter online pornographers and predators from knowingly giving such material to children.

The Supreme Court has consistently ruled that communities may adopt their own standards and implement laws and ordinances accordingly. The decision on the CDA in no way affects community standards, and those standards should be upheld, including at the public library.

2. Isn't the use of blocking software on the Internet censorship?

No. Censorship involves prior restraint by the government of production or distribution of materials. To choose not to stock certain materials is not censorship, but selection, because those materials are still available elsewhere.

The same holds true with the Internet. Blocking software and closed systems allow librarians to select what will, and will not, be made available at the public library.

3. What is the difference between filtering, blocking, and closed systems? Don't they block access to information on breast cancer, AIDS research, works of art, and other materials?

Filtering technology blocks objectionable sites based on key words. This software, which has improved since its introduction, would flag words like *breast* and prevent access to sites including the word.

Blocking technology blocks objectionable sites based on address. The site is flagged based on words; then a human being checks out the site to see if it meets the criteria for pornography. This means that objectionable sites are blocked regardless of what name the pornographer has used, but that legitimate sites are still available. Updates to lists may be obtained every few hours and take only a few seconds. Although filtering and blocking technologies are not 100 percent effective, they provide a valuable layer of protection from harmful material.

Closed systems allow access to materials selected by librarians, and sites outside the system cannot be reached. Although more labor-intensive than blocking, closed systems provide more organized, secure Internet access, and libraries may share their lists of interesting sites.

4. I've heard there is no such thing as server-end blocking. Is this true?

No. Technology is moving at a terrific rate, and there are currently a number of software programs that block at the server level (see appendix B). This means the software is installed on one computer, which acts as a server to other computers on the system, or that blocking is done at the Internet Service Provider level. Server-end blocking prevents individuals from disengaging the blocking software, because the software is not on the individual computers. These programs are also available to individual computers, making them ideal for smaller systems or individuals.

5. Don't adults have a right to view anything they want at the library?

Adults have the right to view anything on the library shelves, but they obviously cannot view any materials the library has chosen not to place on their shelves. If they want to view such materials, they must go elsewhere. By this same token, if an adult wants to view materials the library has chosen not to provide on their computers, they may go elsewhere. Selection on the Internet is consistent with the selection librarians already make of materials they place on their shelves.

Furthermore, libraries should certainly be concerned about the sexually hostile environment created for library employees and patrons by Internet pornography. A number of federal legal precedents have found that pornography was used as a tool in sexual harassment, and libraries would be wise to consider this when they implement their Internet access policies.

Finally, much of the pornography on the Internet appears to meet the Miller test for obscenity, meaning it is prosecutable material. Libraries should be concerned about providing such material to patrons, especially in light of the fact that production and distribution of Internet obscenity are federal crimes, so state exemptions do not apply.

6. Aren't parents responsible for what their children do?

Parents do have the greatest portion of the responsibility for their children, but they cannot be expected to be the sole bearers of that responsibility. Our society has long recognized the need for societal support of parents, which is why we have laws protecting minors, including laws making adult pornography illegal for children in print and broadcast.

Additionally, the rest of society must not neglect children whose parents are not as attentive as they should be. Protecting children requires a partnership among parents, society, and the law.

7. Aren't you asking library staff to baby-sit?

No. Parents should never leave their young children unattended for hours at the library, but they should be able to regard the library as a safe place for children. In the past, libraries were considered a good place for children, and reasonable Internet policies would relieve concerned librarians of the fear that children may be accessing harmful material, or that sexual predators may be contacting children on the Internet.

8. Shouldn't people who don't like pornography just ignore it and let others do what they want?

The problem with pornography, as with many things, is that it affects more than just those who look at it. For some individuals, pornography is progressively addictive in nature. Research shows that pornography affects attitudes, values, and behaviors, and pornography has been linked to sexual crimes against women and children, innocent victims who did not view pornography.

A number of federal legal precedents have found that pornography was used as a tool in sexual harassment. Library boards must implement responsible policies to protect themselves and taxpayers from legal liability.

From *Library Action Manual* (Washington, D.C.: Enough Is Enough, 1997), 7–8.

Appendix D
Pornography on the Internet

When most people hear the word *pornography*, they probably think of the soft-core nudity in *Playboy* magazine. This kind of material would generally fall under the first two categories of pornography called *broadcast indecency* and *harmful to minors* (see definitions at end of appendix D). *Penthouse* and *Hustler* magazines come to mind as well, and they would also be unlawful to exhibit or sell to juveniles. Both of these magazines have had issues found legally obscene in the courts. It is illegal to publicly or commercially disseminate *obscenity*, another category of pornography, under both federal and state laws. Still, both *Penthouse* and *Hustler* have published recent issues where they crossed the line to showing hard-core pictures of penetration clearly visible (PCV), which is content that is clearly prosecutable as obscenity.

Although much of the soft-core material may not be prosecuted as obscenity, and would therefore be available to adults, it is often the gateway to harder material. This is particularly alarming in light of the fact that, according to the 1986 Attorney General's Commission on Pornography, its largest consumers are twelve- to seventeen-year-old boys.[1] Pornographers know that if they can hook this age group when their hormones are raging, these young men could become consumers for life. No longer do men and boys have to sneak away to strip joints or adult bookstores; they can access pornography easily and privately at home, right through the Internet.

While your neighborhood store owners would be arrested for selling or exhibiting even soft-core magazines or videos to minors, there is currently no federal indecency or harmful to minors standard for the Internet. Obscenity laws are not being enforced against hard-core porn being sold on the Web or offered in USENET newsgroups. Although there is joint jurisdiction over enforcement, neither state prosecutors nor federal prosecutors are adequately using the existing obscenity and harmful to minors laws for illegal traffic of online pornography. As a result, peddlers of adult online pornography, much of which is illegal (obscenity) even for adults, are knowingly distributing pornography and live sex images to children without any real fear of prosecution. Since they couldn't care less about who buys their products or who is corrupted in the process, the porn industry and the addicts who distribute it for free will keep polluting cyberspace with pornography until law enforcement agencies step in to clean up the mess. Another way of understanding the pornography industry is to think of it as we would the illegal drug industry. Pornographers push pornography in much the same way as drug pushers push drugs.

Obscenity is limited to hard-core pornography, and its contents include close-ups of graphic sex acts and deviant activities like sexual violence, torture, incest, excretory functions, and bestiality. Production, transmission, and distribution of this material are felonies, yet possession of obscenity in one's home is not a crime. However, use of a phone line or online service to transmit obscenity is a federal crime under current law.

Therefore, it is a felony to either *upload* (transmit from your personal computer to the Internet) or *download* (copy from the Internet onto your personal computer) Internet obscenity.

Because of the subjective nature of current obscenity law, content prosecutable as obscenity is widely available on the Internet, not because it is legal, but because it must be treated as "constitutionally protected" until it has received due process and has been proven illegal in a court of law. Consequently, children have access to content that could be prosecuted as obscenity, such as pictures of women engaged in sexual acts with animals (bestiality).

The fourth category of pornography is *child pornography*. This is material that visually depicts a child under eighteen years old engaged in real or simulated sexual conduct, including lewd or lascivious exhibition of the genitals. Child pornography depicts children in some kind of provocative pose or engaged in some kind of sex act with an adult or another child. When an actual child is violated in child pornography, it is the photographic record of child abuse or a crime in progress.

The Child Pornography Prevention Act of 1996 criminalized the traffic and possession of child pornography that depicts real children or computerized images or altered (morphed) pictures of children engaged in sexual conduct. Since the latter type of material doesn't show a real child being violated, the question has been asked whether it should be treated as child pornography or obscenity. After much debate, Congress determined that whether the child pornography is of an actual child or is computer generated, the effect on the viewer is the same. Its very existence endangers real children due to the way pedophiles and sexual predators use such child sex images to arouse themselves and to seduce children into sexual encounters.

If Some Pornography Is Illegal, Why Is It on the Internet?

Some people believe that the laws regarding pornography can't or shouldn't apply in cyberspace while others feel that the anonymity of the Internet relieves them of responsibility for their actions. Despite many clear-cut U.S. court decisions, child pornography, obscenity, and adult pornography are widely distributed on the Internet. While the U.S. Justice Department has a good record in prosecuting the sexual exploitation of children (i.e., child stalking and child pornography) in cyberspace, no prosecutions exist currently for obscenity on the Internet.[2] Currently, the United States does not have a federal law that makes it illegal to distribute on the Internet indecency or harmful to minors material to children. While there is an abundance of potentially illegal or prosecutable material online, it has yet to be declared obscene by the courts because it hasn't been prosecuted.

The Communications Decency Act (CDA)

The Communications Decency Act of 1996 clarifies that existing federal obscenity laws apply to cyberspace. This means that users who upload or download obscenity or child pornography are violating federal felony statutes. Access providers who knowingly transmit illegal obscenity or child pornography on their boards or services can also be liable. In addition, the CDA contains an important child stalking provision that makes it a crime to use the mail, phones, computers, shippers, Internet, and so on, to engage a minor in prostitution or any sexual act.

In an attempt to close the loophole allowing adult pornography to be distributed to children on the Internet, the CDA extended indecency laws from the airwaves to the cyberspace neighborhood. It was designed to protect children from indecent materials in much the same way that existing federal laws prohibit indecency in broadcasting, cable TV, and dial-a-porn, and in the manner that state laws regulate the display of magazines and films that are harmful to minors.

In June 1997 the U.S. Supreme Court ruled that these indecency provisions of the CDA were unconstitutional. (The obscenity and child stalking provisions were not challenged.) In doing so, the Court held that indecent, but sexually explicit, nonobscene content on the Internet enjoys the full protection of the First Amendment for adults, and, due to the protocols of the Internet in 1996, indecency could not be effectively segregated from minor children. The ruling passes the burden of limiting access to age-inappropriate material on the Internet to parents, teachers, librarians, and other child caregivers. Strong supporters of the CDA, like myself, disagree with the Court's decision, especially with regard to commercial indecency and direct transmission of pornography to children.

During this same week after the Supreme Court's decision, CNN, Gallup, and *USA Today* took a poll in which 94 percent of the people polled said there should be a ban on Internet pornography. Another more recent survey found that 75 percent of the people surveyed said that people should not be allowed to place sexually explicit material on the Internet.[3] While the battle for restricting pornography was lost in the courts, the battle for public awareness of the problem has been successful.

How Can We Legally Protect Children from Pornography without Infringing on the Free Speech Rights of Adults?

Pornographers have found ways to segregate adult pornography from children in print and broadcast, particularly since they have been legally obligated to do so.

The **Children's Online Protection Act** (S.R. 1482 and H.R. 3783) is currently before Congress as of June 1998. This bill would force commercial pornographers on the World Wide Web to require adult verification or use of a credit card for access to their Web site. The intent of the bill is to protect children under 17 from accessing material that is "harmful to minors." This would end the commercial pornographers' practice of placing free "teaser" images on their Web sites, which children are now able to access.

If implemented into law, the Children's Online Protection Act will effectually segregate from children the various types of pornography (harmful to minors, obscenity, and child pornography) currently available for free from U.S. commercial sites on the Web. It will not, however, protect children from exposure to pornography via e-mail, chat rooms, Usenet newsgroups, or commercial Web sites operating outside of the United States. Therefore, all of the safeguards discussed in this book are still applicable and should be implemented to protect kids online. The Children's Online Protection Act is an example of the legal community's role in sharing the responsibility for protecting children on the Internet.

The intent of the law may be realized as it moves through Congress yet before it is signed into law by President Clinton if commercial pornographers begin requiring adult verification before providing any pornographic images on their Web sites.

Enforcement of Existing Laws

Thousands of images on the Internet fit the description of obscenity as established by the Supreme Court, yet the existing Internet obscenity laws are not being enforced and prosecuted. However, by selecting a few strategic abusers of obscenity laws and prosecuting them to the fullest, law enforcement agencies could send a powerful message to pornographers. While we know from experience that proclaiming cocaine illegal doesn't necessarily make the drug problem go away, we do know that severe penalties for those who distribute illegal substances can be an effective deterrent to others. In the same way, uncompromising indictments of Internet pornographers who violate existing obscenity laws could serve as deterrents for the Internet display and distribution of obscenity.

Child pornography laws are being enforced, and I believe that we will see even more aggressive enforcement as more incidents of Internet pedophile activity and child pornography are reported in the media. Yet the challenge to eliminate criminal Internet activity is exacerbated by the global nature of the medium.

A Global Solution

Global access means the necessity of finding a global solution. Whatever I post in Fairfax, Virginia, is immediately accessible everywhere else in the world. This means global standards need to be set and international laws must be enforced worldwide. According to one study, only 31 countries out of the 165 surveyed reported having specific legislation prohibiting the production, distribution, and possession of child pornography.[4] This certainly fuels the international trafficking of child pornography.

No single legislation will work in all global communities. Instead, there must be a harmonization of national laws within regions until laws protecting children become international. As a consequence of the sexual exploitation of children, Interpol, an international law enforcement organization, is organizing a cooperative strategy that represents seventy-seven countries.

Many countries are making great strides in enforcing their own Internet pornography laws. For instance, in 1996 the United Kingdom set up Internet Watch, an organization and hot line that reports illegal USENET postings to the British Police National Criminal Intelligence Service. Internet Watch (http://www.iwf.org.uk) is funded by the British Internet industry.

The Gatekeepers

Many people besides the producers and the distributors are profiting from the pornography industry. The gatekeepers—ISPs and online services—that allow this material to be accessed on their systems stand to make a great deal of money. I have been working for several years in my role at Enough Is Enough to encourage these gatekeepers to comply with existing child pornography and obscenity laws. To do this, they need to remove this content from their proprietary boards and services as well as USENET newsgroups.

Computer Illiteracy in the Law Enforcement Community

Like much of the public, the law enforcement community is not yet "up to speed" on Internet technology, cybercrimes, and the tools to enforce cyberporn laws. I continue to hear of local and state law enforcement agencies that don't even have computers, much less cybercops to police the Net. As for those law enforcement agencies or officials who *are* trained in cyberpolicing, often they don't have the staff or computer resources to devote to Internet crime. Unfortunately, obscenity is globally under-investigated, under-prosecuted, and under-sentenced.

Definitions

child pornography—Material that visually depicts children (real as well as computer-generated) under the age of eighteen engaged in actual or simulated sexual activity, including lewd exhibition of the genitals. Child pornography laws were recently amended to include computerized images or altered (morphed) pictures of children and counterfeit or synthetic images generated by computer that appear to be of real minors or that were marketed or represented to be real child pornography. Laws dealing with child pornography on the Internet are being enforced.

harmful to minors—Material harmful to minors represents nudity or sex that has prurient appeal for minors, is offensive and unsuitable for minors, and lacks serious value for minors. This material, also known as soft-core pornography, is legal for adults, but it is illegal to knowingly sell this material to children under the age of eighteen. There are harmful to minors laws in every state.

indecency—Includes messages or pictures on telephone, radio, or broadcast TV that are patently offensive descriptions or depictions of sexual or excretory organs or activities. This is also known as sexual nudity and "dirty words." There is currently no federal indecency statute that applies to the Internet.

obscenity—Graphic material that focuses on sex and/or sexual violence and is, therefore, prurient, patently offensive, and lacking in serious value. It is often referred to as hard-core pornography and includes close-ups of graphic sex acts and deviant activities, such as penetration, group sex, bestiality, torture, incest, and excretory functions. There are federal and state obscenity laws that forbid transmitting obscenity on the Internet but they have not been vigorously enforced.

Legal Definitions

child pornography—An unprotected visual depiction of a minor child (federal age is under eighteen) engaged in actual or simulated sexual conduct, including a lewd or lascivious exhibition of the genitals. *See New York v Ferber,* 458 U.S. 747 (1982), *Osborne v Ohio,* 495 U.S. 103 (1990), *U.S. v X-Citement Video, Inc.,* 115 S. Ct. 464 (1994). *See also U.S. v Wiegand,* 812 F.2d 1239 (9th Cir. 1987), *cert. denied,* 484 U.S. 856 (1987), *U.S. v Knox,* 32 F.3d 733 (3rd Cir. 1994), *cert. denied,* 115 S. Ct. 897 (1995). Note: In 1996, 18 U.S.C. § 2252A was enacted and § 2256 was amended to include "child pornography" that consists of a visual depiction that "is or appears to be" of an actual minor engaging in sexually explicit conduct. *See Free Speech Coalition v Reno,* No. C-97-0281 SC, *judgment for defendants,* Aug. 12, 1997, *unpublished,* 1997 WL 487758 (N.D. Cal 1997).

obscenity (adult)—Not protected by the First Amendment. The *"Miller* Test" applies to actual or simulated sexual materials and lewd genital exhibitions. *See Miller v California,* 413 U.S. 15, at 24-25 (1973); *Smith v United States,* 431 U.S. 291, at 300-02, 309 (1977); *Pope v Illinois,* 481 U.S. 497, at 500-01 (1987), providing the three-pronged constitutional criteria for federal and state laws and court adjudications:

1. whether the average person, applying contemporary adult community standards, would find that the material, taken as a whole, appeals to a prurient interest in sex (i.e., an erotic, lascivious, abnormal, unhealthy, degrading, shameful, or morbid interest in nudity, sex, or excretion); and
2. whether the average person, applying contemporary adult community standards, would find that the work depicts or describes, in a patently offensive way, sexual conduct (i.e., ultimate sex acts, normal or perverted, actual or simulated; masturbation; excretory functions; lewd exhibition of the genitals; or sadomasochistic sexual abuse); and
3. whether a reasonable person would find that the work, taken as a whole, lacks serious literary, artistic, political, or scientific value.

material harmful to minors—Known as "variable obscenity" or the "*Miller*ized *Ginsberg* Test." *See Ginsberg v New York*, 390 U.S. 629 (1968); and *Miller, Smith, Pope, supra*. It is illegal to sell, exhibit, or display "harmful" ("soft-core") pornography to minor children, even if the material is not obscene or illegal for adults. *See also Com. v Am. Booksellers Ass'n*, 372 S.E.2d 618 (Va. 1988), *followed, American Booksellers Ass'n v Com. of Va.*, 882 F.2d 125 (4th Cir. 1989), *Crawford v Lungren*, 96 F.3d 380 (9th Cir. 1996), *cert. denied*, 117 S. Ct. 1249 (1997). "Harmful to minors" means any written, visual, or audio matter of any kind that:

1. the average person, applying contemporary community standards, would find, taken as a whole and with respect to minors, appeals to a prurient interest in nudity, sex, or excretion, and

2. the average person, applying contemporary community standards, would find depicts, describes, or represents, in a patently offensive way with respect to what is suitable for minors, ultimate sexual acts, normal or perverted, actual or simulated; sadomasochistic sexual acts or abuse; or lewd exhibitions of the genitals, pubic area, buttocks, or post-pubertal female breast, and
3. a reasonable person would find, taken as a whole, lacks serious literary, artistic, political, or scientific value for minors.

broadcast indecency—See *FCC v Pacifica Foundation*, 438 U.S. 726 (1978). The FCC defines broadcast indecency as language or material that, *"in context, depicts or describes in terms patently offensive as measured by contemporary community standards for the broadcast medium, sexual or excretory activities or organs."* *Action For Children's Television v FCC*, 11 F.3d 170, 172 (D.C. Cir. 1993). Enforced by FCC from 6 AM–10 PM. *Action For Children's Television, et al. v F.C.C.*, 58 F.3d 654 (D.C. Cir. 1995), *cert. denied*, 116 S. Ct. 701 (1996).

dial-a-porn—*"The description or depiction of sexual or excretory activities or organs in a patently offensive manner as measured by contemporary community standards for the telephone medium."* Requires: a written request from an adult; or a credit card number; or an adult identification PIN code before transmission. *See Sable Communications of California, Inc. v FCC*, 492 U.S. 115, 126, 128-30 (1989); *Information Providers' Coalition v FCC*, 928 F.2d 866, 872 (9th Cir. 1991); *Dial Information Services Corporation of New York v Thornburgh*, 938 F.2d 1535 (2nd Cir. 1991), *cert. denied*, 502 U.S. 1072 (1992).

cable indecency—Cable operators may refuse to carry indecent leased access programming that the operator reasonably believes *"describes or depicts sexual or excretory activities or organs in a patently offensive manner as measured by contemporary community standards for the cable medium."* Cable operators who choose to carry indecent programming on leased access channels are not required to place such programs on a separate, blocked channel. *See Denver Area Ed. Tel. Consort. v FCC*, 116 S. Ct. 2374 (1996). *See also Playboy Entertainment Group v United States*, 945 F. Supp. 772 (D. Del. 1996), *aff'd*, 117 S. Ct. 1309 (1997) (upholding CDA's cable indecency provisions).

computer "Internet" indecency—The Communications Decency Act of 1996 ("CDA"), 110 Stat. 133-43, amended 47 U.S.C. § 223 to add a new subsection 223 (d) to prohibit knowingly sending or displaying "indecent" material to minors under age 18 by computer and defined the indecency which is unlawful to provide to minors as: *"any comment, request, suggestion, proposal, image, or other communication that, in context, depicts or describes, in terms patently offensive as measured by contemporary community standards, sexual or excretory activities or organs."* See *Joint Explanatory Statement of the Committee of Conference* ("Conference Report on the CDA"), 1996 U.S.C.C.A.N. Leg. Hist., at 200-11. The indecency provisions for interactive computer systems were held unenforceable in *Reno v ACLU*, 117 S. Ct. 2329 (1997), but the Court reaffirmed the application of obscenity and child pornography laws in "cyberspace."

pornography—A generic term that can refer to materials that are either "legal" or "illegal" to disseminate under the circumstances. "Pornography" encompasses all sexually oriented material intended primarily to arouse the reader, viewer, or listener. *See Webster's Dictionary; Miller v California*, 413 U.S. 15, 18 n. 2 (1973); *Final Report*, Attorney General's Commission on

Pornography (1986), Chapter One, "Defining our Central Terms." Serious works of art, literature, politics, or science; "mere nudity," medical works, even though they deal with sex or include sexual references or depictions, would not be considered "pornography" in the context of their legitimate uses. On the other hand, since obscenity can include both actual and simulated conduct, all "Hard-Core Pornography" that depicts penetration clearly visible ("PCV") is "implicitly" within the application of the constitutional criteria of the Supreme Court's obscenity test. *See Mishkin v New York*, 383 U.S. 506, 508 (1966), *Miller v California*, 413 U.S. 15, 29 (1973).

For more information, see B. Taylor, "Hard-core Pornography: A Proposal for a Per-se Rule," 21 U. Mich. J. L. Ref. 255 (1988).

Legal definitions from National Law Center for Children and Families, 4103 Chain Bridge Rd. #410, Fairfax, VA 22030-4105, 703-691-4626, fax: 703-691-4669. Used by permission.

Appendix E
Sample House Rules

The following are samples of House Rules for Internet use.

Family Internet Rules

1. I will not tell anyone on the Internet my full name, address, telephone number, or the name of my school without my parents' permission.
2. I will remember that some kids I meet in chat rooms may not really be kids. Sometimes bad people pretend to be kids in chat rooms.
3. I will not meet in person for the first time with any of my online friends unless it is in a public place and my father or mother is with me.
4. I will do to others as I would have them do to me. I will never send out mean messages nor will I respond with mean messages to any that are sent to me.
5. I will stop immediately if I come across anything that makes me feel uncomfortable. It is not my fault if I see something bad accidentally. If I do see

something inappropriate, I will get offline or turn off my computer. I then will tell my parents what happened.

6. I will not go online over (set an amount of time) per week.
7. I will follow my family's guidelines for net safety.

Signed _____

(Have all family members sign here.)

Date _____

From Zachary Britton, *SafetyNet* (Eugene, Ore.: Harvest House, 1998), 56–57. Used by permission.

Family Internet Safety Pact

1. I UNDERSTAND there is some danger online; criminals roam the Internet just as they roam the streets.
2. I UNDERSTAND that some people online pretend to be someone they are not. They can lie about their age, sex, interests, personality, job, everything and anything.
3. I UNDERSTAND that some people online try to befriend kids who aren't getting along with their parents.
4. I UNDERSTAND that private family matters should not be discussed online. Instead, I should talk about them with a trusted adult.
5. I UNDERSTAND that my parents may spot-check my time online, because they love me and want to ensure my safety!
6. I WILL NOT give out my full name online.
7. I WILL NOT give out my home address online.
8. I WILL NOT give out my phone number online.
9. I WILL NOT give out the name or location of the school I attend while online.

10. I WILL NOT go alone to meet in person someone I know only from online.
11. If I really want to meet an online acquaintance, I WILL
    • Get permission from my parents or guardian(s)
    • Meet the person in a public place
    • Take along my parent(s) or a group of friends
12. I WILL report to my parents any X-rated e-mail, images, or files that are sent to me via the Internet.

_____   _____
Child's Signature   Parent's Signature

_____   _____
Date   Date

Appendix F
PICSRules

The World Wide Web Consortium has recently proposed a new specification document. The new document describes PICSRules, a format that will make it easy for filtering products to include installable configurations. Future products are expected to use PICSRules in two ways:

- One-click installation of filtering settings. For example, a local PTA chapter could create a Web site with recommended settings for various age groups, expressed as PICSRules. A parent could click on a link at that Web site, and automatically configure his or her home computer to use those recommended settings.
- Sorted and filtered searches. When conducting a search, a user's computer could send a PICSRule to a search engine and the search engine would then send back only links that match the criteria in the PICSRule. For example, when searching on the word "toy," the search engine could send back only links to sites dealing with children's toys and not those sites selling sex toys.

For information online:

- Resnick, Paul. "Filtering Information on the Internet," *Scientific American* (March 1997), 106–8. Available online at http://www.sciam.com/0397issue/0397 resnick.html.
- The PICS home page: http://www.w3.org/PICS.
- The PICS and Intellectual Freedom FAQ: http://www .si.umich.edu/~presnick/pics/intfree/FAQ.htm.

From Lorrie Faith Cranor and Paul Resnick, *Technology Inventory*, 10.

Appendix G
Internet Acceptable-Use Policies

Colorado Springs Christian School— Middle School

The Colorado Springs Christian Middle School believes that the Internet has much to offer students with its wide variety of resources. It is our goal to educate students about efficient, ethical, and appropriate use of those resources. Within the context of our mission statement as a school, the Internet connection will be used to meet the goals in our curriculum. Specifically, students will have the opportunity to enhance their learning through:

1. a wealth of additional resources for reference and research.
2. consulting with experts in a variety of fields.
3. communicating with other students and individuals in areas or situations they are studying.
4. learning to conduct searches, evaluate resources, and locate relevant material, and
5. interacting with up-to-date primary sources.

In order to assist students in learning to use the Internet correctly, the school will do everything it can to insure that students access the resources appropriately. This includes providing:

1. a reliable connection that is protected by the best censorware we can find. Censorware blocks sites that are objectionable for content, language, or a variety of other things that the school has defined as inappropriate, such as releasing personal information.
2. supervision of students while they are using the Internet. The Internet connection will be disabled whenever there will not be adequate supervision. (Our censorware can do this for us.)
3. training for students (and parents) that clearly spells out what is appropriate and what is inappropriate. Students will be given general instruction about what is available on the Internet and how they can find what they are looking for through searches, how to save, and how to print. They will also receive instruction in Netiquette and proper citing and evaluation of sources.
4. an "Internet license" (or validation stamp on the student's ID) will be issued that allows only students who have successfully passed the training to use the Internet independently. Involved in the application for the license will be the student's and parents' agreements to abide by the Internet policies of the school. Expectations will be clearly spelled out, and students will be aware of what constitutes a violation.

Note: Occasionally, whole classes with their teachers will use the Internet as one of many tools in the research process. If the student has not gained an Internet license, he/she will always be under the direct supervision of a teacher or librarian. No student will be allowed to use the Internet without the censorware in place unless under the direct supervision of the teacher for specific research. (Example: sites with tobacco or alcohol would be censored, but a student doing a report on such a topic would be able to access appropriate materials with a teacher present. . . . Students without the Internet license cannot use the Internet on days that the technology coordinator is not present. Students with the Internet license could also use the Internet when the librarian or another teacher is supervising.

It is to be understood that Internet access for students is a privilege, not a right. All users of the Internet will agree to adhere to the following Code of Ethics:

I will strive to act in all situations with honesty, integrity, and respect for the rights of others and to help others to behave in a similar fashion. I will make a conscious effort to be a good testimony to my fellow students, faculty members, and others I communicate with on the Internet. I agree to follow Colorado Springs Christian School's basic rules. I will strive to apply Philippians 4:8 to my electronic communication. "Finally, brothers, whatever is true, whatever is noble, whatever is right, whatever is pure, whatever is lovely, whatever is admirable—if anything is excellent or praiseworthy— think about such things."

The Internet user is held responsible for his/her actions whenever using the Internet. Unacceptable uses of the network will result in the suspension or revoking of these privileges. Some examples of unacceptable use are:

1. using the network for any illegal activity
2. using the network for financial gain or initiating any financial transactions
3. degrading or disrupting the equipment or system performance. Any security problems must be reported to the technology coordinator and not shared with other users
4. vandalizing the data of another user
5. wastefully using finite resources, after being warned and instructed as to proper use
6. gaining unauthorized access to resources, including attempting to get around the censorware installed on a computer with Internet access
7. invading the privacy of individuals including reading mail that belongs to others without their permission
8. using an account owned by another user—with or without that user's permission
9. posting personal communications without the author's consent or posting information not meant to be made public
10. posting rude or inappropriate messages
11. downloading viruses or attempting to circumvent virus protection programs
12. violating the spirit of the Colorado Springs Christian School's Mission Statement.

By signing the consent and waiver form attached, the student agrees to abide by these restrictions. The student and parent (or guardian) must sign after they have discussed these rights and responsibilities together.

The Internet user and his/her parents must understand that he/she uses the Internet at his/her own risk. Considering the provisions mentioned above, CSCS cannot assume responsibility for:

1. the reliability of the content of a source received by a user. Students must evaluate and cite sources appropriately.
2. costs that the students incur if they request a product or service for a fee.
3. any consequences of disruption in service that may result in lack of resources. Though every effort will be made to insure a reliable connection, there may be times when the Internet service is down or scheduled for use by teachers, classes, or other students.
4. guaranteeing privacy of mail. Though we do support privacy of e-mail, users must not assume that this is guaranteed. The technology coordinator and the principal reserve the right to investigate possible misuses or to monitor any e-mail that comes through CSCS computers.

Student's Section

I have read CSCS's Acceptable-Use Policy for the Internet. I agree to follow the rules contained in this policy. I understand that if I violate the rules, my privileges can be terminated and I may face other disciplinary measures. I agree to use the Internet according to the code of ethics contained in the Acceptable-Use Policy.

User Name _____   Grade _____
Signature _____   Date _____

Parent's Section

If you would like your son or daughter to receive an Internet license, please sign the following waiver:

As a parent or legal guardian of the student signing above, I have read this Internet Acceptable-Use Policy and grant permission for my son or daughter to access the Internet. I understand that the school's computing resources are designed for educational purposes. I also understand that there is unacceptable and controversial material on the Internet that might be accessed despite all the precautions. I understand that my son or daughter will be held liable for violations of this policy.

Parent's Name _____
Daytime Phone _____
Signature _____ Date _____

See Erin Wilcox, "Establishing An Internet Policy For Your School," *ACSI Legal/Legislative Update* (fall 1997), 9–10.

Model Policy on Internet Sexual Harassment

© Colonel Richard H. Black (USA Ret.),
October 16, 1997
11051 Judicial Drive, Fairfax, VA 22030

Note: This policy was implemented by the Loudoun County Libraries, but a lawsuit by a group called Mainstream Loudoun, backed by the ACLU, is now pending against it. The lawsuit challenges the constitutionality of the policy. Colonel Black was quite clever to move the issue from content regulation to sexually hostile environment issues. Whatever the outcome of this lawsuit, it will have tremendous impact on library communities across the nation.

General

1. Title VII of the Civil Rights Act prohibits sex discrimination. Library pornography can create a sexually hostile environment for patrons or staff. Pornographic Internet displays may intimidate patrons or staff, denying them equal access to public facilities. Such displays would transform the library environment from one of reading and scholarship to one which invites unwelcome sexual advances and sexual harassment. Permitting pornographic displays may constitute unlawful sex discrimination in violation of Title VII of the Civil Rights Act. This policy seeks to prevent Internet sexual harassment.
2. Historically, the library has not selected mere pornography for book, magazine, or video collections. It will not do so through the Internet.

Internet Services Provided

The Internet will be accessible as follows:
1. E-mail, chat rooms, and pornography will not be provided;
2. Site blocking software will be installed on all computers. To the extent technically feasible, such software will:
   a. Block child pornography and obscene material (hard-core pornography)
   b. Block material deemed Harmful to Juveniles under applicable (State) statutes and legal precedents (soft-core pornography). Public access to such material could create an unlawful, sexually hostile environment, and might incite dangerous criminal misconduct.

3. Internet computers will be installed in close proximity to, and in full view of, library staff in order to:
   a. Discourage efforts to override blocking software; and,
   b. Provide patrons a secure environment against sexual harassment when using the Internet.
4. Patrons will not be permitted to use the Internet to access pornography. Persons using the Internet to access material in paragraph 2, will be told they are violating the Policy on Internet Sexual Harassment. If they continue, they will be told to leave the library. If they refuse, they will be considered in trespass, and police may be called to remove them. Children's parents will also be notified unless the child obeys the first request to stop.

Children

1. Because blocking software may not be completely effective, parents will be accorded the maximum control over children's Internet access.
2. Parents or guardians must give written permission for children under age 18 to access the Internet. Parents or guardians must personally appear and show proof of identity before filling out the access form, and personally present it to library staff. Children's library cards will be overstamped to verify parental permission to use the Internet. Parents may revoke children's access for any reason.

Severability

If a court overrules a provision of this policy, remaining portions remain in effect.

Forms

The attached forms will be used.

Parent Permission Acknowledgment for Children 17 Years of Age and Under

1. As a parent or legal guardian of the minor child listed below, I give permission for my child to access the Internet. I understand that my child's access to library materials is my sole responsibility and prerogative.
2. I understand that I may revoke this permission at any time by returning my child's library card so he or she can have a card issued without Internet access.
3. As a user of the library's Internet, I have read and will abide by the above agreement.

Parent's name (print) _____

Parent's signature _____Date _____

Child's name (print) _____

Child's signature _____

Address _____

_____

_____

Phone _____Date_____

From Enough Is Enough, *Library Action Manual,* 25–28.

Model Internet Use Policy for Public Libraries

Library Mission

1. The _____ Public Library's mission is to provide knowledge, inspiration, and enjoyment for all.
2. Its aim is to promote the value of information, reflecting the diversity of culture and viewpoints, and to enhance the community's awareness of services that aid in the development of individual and community creativity and excellence.

General Policies

1. In support of its mission and in response to advancing technology, the _____ Public Library offers the community access to the Internet. The library system does not provide public access to electronic mail or access to news/USENET and discussion/IRC groups.
2. The Internet is, in general, an unregulated medium. Information on the Internet is not necessarily current, accurate, or complete. While much valuable information is posted on the Internet, some is obscene or is child pornography as defined by other applicable state law or may otherwise be harmful or inappropriate. The library system attempts to balance the desire for free access to varying information sources against the need to avoid material that unlawfully violates community standards as defined by applicable state law, creates a hostile environment for patron and/or staff, or is obscene.

Guidelines for Use of the Internet on Library Computers

1. Guidelines detailing the specific procedures for scheduling use of the Internet will be available at your local library.
2. All users of the Internet are expected to use these resources in a responsible manner, consistent with the educational and informational purposes for which they are provided, and to follow these policies.
3. Data downloaded from the Internet must comply with copyright law.
4. Downloaded data may contain viruses. Users may wish to maintain current virus-checking software to protect their home computer systems. The library system is not responsible for damage to any user's disks, computers, or data caused by the use of library computers.
5. Customers may not use personal software on library computers.
6. All library Internet access computers are equipped with screening software that attempts to filter obscene materials and child pornography. However, consistent with the educational and informational purposes for which they are provided, an adult patron may obtain unfiltered access for personal use for a specific session. Patrons are not permitted to knowingly access, upload, or download hard-core pornography or child pornography.
7. To the extent possible, computers providing Internet access will be placed in full public view of the library staff to discourage inappropriate use.

Children's Use of the Internet

1. Parents and guardians are responsible for determining the limits of their children's access to the Internet. Library staff are not responsible for ensuring that children access only appropriate materials on the Internet. Parents and children are encouraged to read "Child Safety on the Information Highway," published by the National Center for Missing and Exploited Children and the Interactive Services Association, which provides valuable tips about Internet safety for children.

2. All library computers are equipped with screening software to limit access to material that unlawfully violates community standards of decency, as defined by applicable state law, creates a hostile work environment for our staff or our patrons, or exposes those of tender age to violent or sexually explicit text and imagery. Available screening software cannot completely eliminate all such material. Parents and guardians must understand that the libraries cannot ensure that a child will not purposefully or inadvertently access such materials, and should supervise their children accordingly.

3. As with all library materials, restrictions on a child's access is the sole responsibility and prerogative of his or her parents or guardians. They are encouraged to develop rules for their children's use of the Internet.

4. CUSTOMERS 17 YEARS OF AGE AND UNDER MAY OBTAIN UNFILTERED INTERNET ACCESS ONLY WHEN A PARENT OR LEGAL GUARDIAN IS PHYSICALLY PRESENT FOR THE DURATION OF THAT SPECIFIC SESSION.

Adapted from Enough Is Enough, *Library Action Manual*, 1997.

Appendix H
Third-Party Labels from Values-Oriented Organizations

Quite a few third party labeling services are available when we include PICS-based services along with those packaged with filtering software, such as Net Nanny, SurfWatch, or Bess. Values-oriented organizations, both religious and secular, are a potential source for labels that represent diverse viewpoints. The PTA, the Scouts, a church, or perhaps even an organization like the AARP could rise to the challenge of coordinating all the volunteer labor needed to engage in the project of labeling. It could be a great service not only to children, but to adults as well. Net Shepherd has coordinated a volunteer effort to label more than 1.3 million URLs, representing over five hundred thousand Web sites.

From Lorrie Faith Cranor and Paul Resnick, *Technology Inventory*, 8.

Appendix I
American Civil Liberties Union Policy Number 4

Censorship of Obscenity, Pornography, and Indecency

(a) The ACLU opposes any restraint on the right to create, publish or distribute materials to adults, or the right of adults to choose the materials they read or view, on the basis of obscenity, pornography or indecency. Freedom of speech and press and freedom to read can be safeguarded effectively only if the First Amendment is applied strictly—to prohibit any restriction on these basic rights. In pursuing this policy, the ACLU emphasizes that it is neither urging the circulation nor evaluating the merit of such material.

(b) Laws which punish the distribution or exposure of such materials to minors violate the First Amendment, and inevitably restrict the right to publish and distribute such materials to adults. The complex social problems which prompt such statutes cannot be solved by limiting freedom of speech and press and avoiding the real causes.

The ACLU is well aware of the concern of parents, clergy and community officials about the exposure of children to what many regard as hard-core pornography, whether through its availability at neighborhood stores and newsstands or by its unsolicited dissemination through the mails. However, the Union maintains that a causal relationship between exposure to sexually explicit material and juvenile delinquency has never been carried to the point of definitive proof. (See policy on Comic Books.) As a practical matter it would appear that there can be no substitute for parental responsibility. Inevitably, any legal sanctions would threaten the distribution of non-pornographic materials.

(c) The ACLU has long maintained that all definitions of obscenity are meaningless because this type of judgment is inevitably subjective and personal. Courts and juries continue to differ over what constitutes obscenity, often including in that category materials that have won worldwide acclaim.

The standard that to be judged obscene a work must lack "serious literary, artistic, political or social value" is imprecise and uncertain. It is impossible to draw the exact line between "important" and "worthless" material because the informed, critical community is itself just as often divided on the issue of the social importance as on the "appeal to prurient interest" of any given work. Attempts to define "obscenity" frequently result in condemning most severely expression of a controversial nature—the very kind of speech for whose protection the First Amendment was written.

(d) The ACLU believes that the constitutional guarantees of free speech and press apply to all expression and that all limitations of expression on the grounds of obscenity, pornography or indecency are unconstitutional. But so long as courts sustain such limitations in any form, it will also work to minimize their restrictive effect. Under the First Amendment and the due process clause of the Fifth Amendment, such statutes should be required to define precisely the forms of proscribed speech, provide strict procedural safeguards, and choose the least restrictive methods of regulation.

The following safeguards for freedom of expression should be required:

1) Any statutory definition of obscenity must be drawn precisely and narrowly.
2) Creators, publishers and producers, their distributors, exhibitors and retailers, should not be threatened with the sanctions of criminal statutes for distributing or being connected with a work before it has been determined obscene in an adversary civil proceeding with a standard of proof of clear and convincing evidence. The state should be required to select a civil proceeding, as the least restrictive method of censorship.
3) Obscenity statutes should provide for prompt trials, determination and appellate review within specified time periods; and to require proof of scienter under clearly defined and reasonable standards.
4) Obscenity statutes should assure defendants the right to counsel; and if a defendant is acquitted, the defendant should be entitled to recover the costs and reasonable attorneys' fees incurred in defending the person's First Amendment rights.
5) Creators, publishers and producers, their distributors, exhibitors and retailers, should not be submitted to harassment by a multiplicity of proceedings. The state should not be entitled to subject a

work to more than one civil proceeding to determine its obscenity. This could be accomplished either by requiring that its Attorney General institute such proceeding (or designate a district or county attorney to do so), or by providing that once an obscenity proceeding has been commenced in a state against a work, no other proceeding may be instituted against the same work in other counties, cities or towns until and unless there has been a final judgment that the work is obscene. (For the due process aspects of obscenity hearings in the broadcast media, see policy on Diversity, Censorship, and FCC Regulation.)

6) Distributors, exhibitors and retailers should not be obliged to risk punishment by misjudging the age of a minor. Such persons should not be required to keep records of evidence submitted by minors; and should be entitled to rely reasonably on a minor's statement of age.

7) There should not be a variable standard of obscenity for minors. [Board Minutes, April 13–14, 1985.]

(e) The ACLU opposes all zoning plans restricting the availability of books, movies and other communications media because of their content. The ACLU has long opposed any restraint on the dissemination of materials on grounds of obscenity. It therefore believes that zoning plans designed to regulate so-called pornographic materials comprise another form of restraint that impinges on constitutionally protected speech. The breadth of zoning ordinances inevitably inhibits the full and free exchange of information and expression. [Board Minutes, June 18–19, 1977, April 13–14, 1985.]

(f) Statutes that restrict pornography on the ground that it contributes to the subordination of women violate the free press and free speech guarantees of the First Amendment. The ACLU opposes any form of sex discrimination against women or men, but censoring speech will in the end lead to more intolerance, not less.

Proponents of such statutes contend that pornography is a form of sex discrimination because it reinforces an inferior image of women and thus harms women's status. They argue that pornography also leads to physical abuse of women, by increasing male aggression towards them; also that actresses and models are often physically and psychologically abused in the actual production of pornographic movies and photographs, typically by being coerced into sex.

Pornography, however, is speech; it is not conduct. Certain pornographic materials may be offensive to some and perhaps most Americans. Yet many publications and films which broad segments of the public may wish to see or read, ranging from current cultural expression to renowned works of art, could be construed as pornography and face restriction under these statutes.

Some assert that there is "scientific proof" showing an actual causal relationship between viewing of pornography and anti-social behavior. The ACLU believes, however, that no different test of the effects of speech is applicable in this area as in any other area.

Much expression may offend the sensibilities of people and indeed have a harmful effect on some. But this is no reason to sacrifice the First Amendment. The First Amendment does not allow suppression of speech because of the potential harm.

Society, moreover, has ample means other than suppression for dealing with the types of harm that some contend are caused or aggravated by pornography. Enforcement of criminal laws regarding assault, coerced sex, kidnapping and trespassing; strengthening of rape laws including elimination of the "spousal rape" exception under which husbands may not be prosecuted for raping their wives; enforcement of Title VII (of the Civil Rights Act of 1964) and other sex discrimination laws are legitimate remedies. Victims of sexual offenses may also have grounds to sue for damages for torts or contract claims. [Board Minutes, April 13–14, 1985.]

(g) The ACLU believes that the First Amendment protects the dissemination of all forms of communication. The ACLU opposes on First Amendment grounds laws that restrict the production and distribution of any printed and visual materials even when some of the producers of those materials are punishable under criminal law.

The ACLU views the use of children in the production of visual depictions of sexually explicit conduct as a violation of children's rights when such use is highly likely to cause: (a) substantial physical harm or, (b) substantial and continuing emotional or psychological harm. Government quite properly has the means to protect the interests of children in these situations by the use of criminal prosecution of those persons who are likely to cause such harm to children. [Board Minutes, June 12, 1985.]

Courtesy of the American Civil Liberties Union (ACLU), 125 Broad Street, New York, NY 10004, 215-549-2500, http://www.aclu.org.

Notes

Chapter 1: Bridging the Technogeneration Gap

1. Bill Clinton, "A Message to Parents about the Internet," in *Parents Guide to the Internet* (Washington, D.C.: U.S. Department of Education, November 1997), cover letter.

2. "Internet Connections Reach 82 Million PCs Worldwide," *The Washington Times*, 28 August 1997, p. A2.

3. Richard Riley, remarks made at Internet/Online Summit: Focus on Children, Washington, D.C., 2 December 1997.

4. Wendy Lazarus and Laurie Lipper, *The Parents' Guide to the Information Superhighway* (Washington, D.C.: The Children's Partnership with the National PTA and National Urban League, 1998), 3.

5. The sections on the vocabulary of computers and the explanation of the Internet are adapted from *Parents Guide to the Internet*, 1–2.

6. Ibid., 2.

7. "Children and the Internet" (prepared by Children Now on behalf of Center for Media Education, Children Now, Children's Defense Fund, Children's Partnership, American Academy of Pediatrics, National Association of Elementary School Principals), 1.

8. Kathryn C. Montgomery, *Creating an Electronic Legacy for Our Children* (Washington, D.C.: Center for Media Education, 1997), 8–9.

9. "Children and the Internet," 3.

10. Parry Aftab, *A Parent's Guide to the Internet* (New York: SC Press, 1997), 100.

11. Stephen J. Kavanagh, *Protecting Children in Cyberspace* (Springfield, Va.: Behavioral Psychotherapy Center, 1997), 35–37, 47–48.

12. Montgomery, *Creating an Electronic Legacy*, 8.

13. Patrice M. Jones, "Internet Term Papers Write New Chapter on Plagiarism," *Chicago Tribune*, 8 December 1997, sec. 1, p. 1.

14. Cornelia Grumman, "Webaholics," *Chicago Tribune*, 26 June 1996 at *http://chicago.tribune.com*.

Chapter 2: For Net-Shy Parents—Internet 101

1. Some of the information in this chapter is adapted from *Parents Guide to the Internet*, 2–8.

Chapter 3: The Serious Risks of Cyberspace

1. *Washington Post*, quoting *Interactive Weekly*, 30 March 1997, p. C4.

2. "Protecting Your Family in Cyberspace," *NCPCF in Action Special Report* (Cincinnati, Ohio: National Coalition of Children & Families, November 1997), 2.

3. John Simons, "The Web's Dirty Secret," *U.S. News & World Report*, 19 August 1996, 52.

4. Based on information given to Enough Is Enough via telephone conversations with X-Stop and Sterling Solutions, two blocking software companies.

5. Randall E. Stross, "The Cyber Vice Squad," *U.S. News & World Report*, 17 March 1997, 45.

6. "WebChaperone Fact Sheet," WebCo International, 1997.

7. Tod Lindberg, "Unmolested Molesters," *Weekly Standard*, 14 April 1997, 18.

8. Laura J. Lederer, *National Legislation on and International Trafficking in Child Pornography*, 2d ed. (Minneapolis: Center on Speech, Equality, and Harm, University of Minnesota, 1997), 1.

9. Posted 2 July 1997 at *Penthouse*'s home page: http://www.penthousemag.com.

10. Ibid., 11.

11. Susan Clary, "2 Teens Charged in Computer Porn Case," *St. Petersburg Times*, 21 May 1996, p. 3B.

12. GRIP Student Opinion Responses, 5 December 1997.

13. *Take Action Manual* (Washington, D.C.: Enough Is Enough, 1995–96), 57.

14. Laura J. Lederer, *National Legislation on and International Trafficking in Child Pornography*, 2d ed. (Minneapolis: University of Minnesota Center on Speech, Equality, and Harm, 1997), 1.

15. Ibid.

16. See "The Agincourt Project," a White Paper on Internet Pornography: An Action Proposal for the Elimination of Illegal Pornography and Child Pornography from the Internet (presented at OCAF [Oklahomans for Children and Families], Oklahoma City, 1996) at www.ocaf.org and www.nccip.org.

17. Thomas E. Weber, "The X Files," *Wall Street Journal*, 20 May 1997, A1.

18. Press release, U.S. Department of Justice, 16 July 1996.

19. Joanne von Alroth, "Internet 'Pal' Raped Teen in Wheelchair, Court Told," *Chicago Tribune*, 11 December 1997, sec. 2, p. 7.

20. Suzanne Fields, "The Internet Isn't Child Friendly," *Washington Times*, 29 May 1997, A19.

21. Phil Long, "High-tech Pedophiles," *Miami Herald*, 31 December 1995.

22. Judd Gregg, "Child Pornography and the Internet: What Every Parent, Teacher, and Child Should Know," prepared by the office of Senator Judd Gregg of New Hampshire, Washington, D.C.

Chapter 4: Shedding Light on the Darkness of Pornography

1. Much of the material on myths in this chapter was adapted from *Take Action Manual*, 15–18.

2. See letter from Robert H. Macy, district attorney, Oklahoma County, Oklahoma.

3. J. H. Court, "Pornography and Sex Crimes," *International Journal of Criminology and Penology* 5 (1977), 129–57, quoted in Victor B. Cline, *Pornography's Effects on Adults and Children* (New York: Morality in Media, 1990).

4. Cline, *Pornography's Effects*, 8.

5. W. L. Marshall, "The Use of Sexually Explicit Stimuli by Rapists, Child Molesters, and Nonoffenders," *The Journal of Sex Research* 25, no. 2 (May 1988): 267–88.

6. See H. J. Eysenck, "Robustness of Experimental Support for the General Theory of Desensitization," in Neil M. Malamuth and Edward Donnerstein, eds., *Pornography and Sexual Aggression* (Orlando, Fla.: Academic Press, 1984), 314. D. Zillmann, "Effects of Prolonged Consumption of Pornography," in *Pornography: Research Advances and Policy Considerations*, eds. D. Zillman and J. Bryant (Hillsdale, N.J.: Erlbaum, 1989), 129.

7. *Take Action Manual*, 9.

8. Neil Postman, *The Disappearance of Childhood* (New York: Vintage, 1994), 137.

9. Tom Minnery, *Pornography: A Human Tragedy* (Wheaton: Tyndale House).

10. *Facts in Brief* (The Alan Buttmacher Institute, 1994).

11. Cline, *Pornography's Effects*, 2–3.

12. K. E. Davis and G. N. Braucht, *Exposure to Pornography, Character and Sexual Deviance*, Technical Reports of the Commission on Obscenity and Pornography (1970), 7.

13. Patrick Carnes, *Don't Call It Love: Recovery from Sexual Addictions* (New York: Bantam, 1991).

14. Zillman, "Effects of Prolonged Consumption of Pornography," 129.

15. Daniel Linz, "Exposure to Sexually Explicit Materials and Attitudes toward Rape," *Journal of Sex Research* 26, no. 1 (February 1989): 50–84.

16. Donald M. Joy, *Re-Bonding: Preventing and Restoring Damaged Relationships* (Dallas: Word, 1986), 95.

17. Dianne Smith, "When My Worst Fear Came True," *Focus on the Family* (July 1993), 10–11.

18. Kavanagh, *Protecting Children in Cyberspace*, 58–59.

19. Cline, *Pornography's Effects*, 11.

20. Edward Donnerstein, "Ordinances to Add Pornography to Discrimination against Women," statement at Public Hearing of Minneapolis City Council Session (12 December 1983). See also Luis T. Garcia, "Exposure to Pornography and Attitudes about Women and Rape: A Correlative Study," AG 22 (1986), 382–83. This study found "subjects with a greater degree of exposure to violent sexual materials tended to believe that: (a) women are responsible for preventing their own rape, (b) rapists should not be severely punished, and (c) women should not resist a rape attack. In addition, researchers found that exposure to

violent sexual material correlated significantly with the belief that rapists are normal. See also Zillman, "Effects of Prolonged Consumption," 129; and N. Malamuth and J. Ceniti, 129–37. "Study . . . results consistently showed a relationship between one's reported likelihood to rape and responses associated with convicted rapists such as sexual arousal to rape stimuli, callous attitudes toward rape, beliefs in the rape myths, and hostility towards women."

21. Cline, *Pornography's Effects*, 8.

22. Gene McConnell, "Pornography Equals Sex and Power and Violence," *Christian Counseling Today* (Fall 1996), 33.

23. Gary R. Brooks, *The Centerfold Syndrome: How Men Can Overcome Objectification and Achieve Intimacy with Women* (San Francisco, Calif.: Jossey-Bass, 1996), 2.

24. Cline, *Pornography's Effects*, 11.

25. Kavanagh, "Protecting Children in Cyberspace," 58–59.

26. Cline, *Pornography's Effects*, 7; see also James L. McGaugh, "Preserving the Presence of the Past," *American Psychologist 161* (1983), 38. McGaugh concludes that human memory is formed in part by the release of the chemical epinephrine, which, upon emotional arousal, leaves behind an imprint on the brain.

27. Interview with Ann Burgess, professor of nursing, University of Pennsylvania, 15 January 1997. "Pornography—Victims and Perpetrators," Symposium on Media Violence & Pornography, Proceedings Resource Book and Research Guide, ed. D. Scott (1984).

28. Cynthia Monahon, *Children and Trauma* (San Francisco: Jossey-Bass, 1993), 45.

29. Jerry Bergman, Ph.D., "The Influence of Pornography on Sexual Development: Three Case Histories," *Family Therapy* IX, no. 3 (1982): 265.

30. McConnell, "Pornography Equals Sex and Power," 33.

31. Cline, *Pornography's Effects*, 3–5.

32. Victor B. Cline, "Pornography and Sexual Addictions," *Christian Counseling Today* 4, no. 4 (1996): 58.

33. Cline, *Pornography's Effects*, 4.

34. From Kavanagh, *Protecting Children in Cyberspace*, 63–65.

35. R. S. Pynoos and S. Eth, "Children Traumatized by Witnessing Acts of Personal Violence: Homicide, Rape, or Suicide Behavior," in *Post-Traumatic Stress Disorder in Children*, eds. S. Eth and R. S. Pynoos (Washington, D.C.: American Psychiatric Press, 1985), 17–44.

36. Monahon, *Children and Trauma*, 45.

37. Adapted from *Take Action Manual*, 52.

Chapter 5: The First Line of Defense

1. Kavanagh, *Protecting Children in Cyberspace*, 80.

2. Aftab, *A Parent's Guide to the Internet*, 126–27.

3. Adapted from Lazarus and Lipper, *The Parents' Guide to the Information Superhighway*, 5–7.

4. Laura E. Berk, *Infants, Children, and Adolescents* (Needham Heights, Mass.: Allyn & Bacon, 1993), 488.

5. "Web of Deception: Threats to Children from Online Marketing" (Center for Media Education: Wash-

ington, D.C., 1996) at http://epn.org/cme/cmwdecov.html.

6. Lawrence J. Magid, *Teen Safety on the Information Highway* (Arlington, Va.: National Center for Missing and Exploited Children, 1998), 2.

7. Adapted from Robert G. De Moss Jr., *Learn to Discern* (Grand Rapids: Zondervan, 1992).

8. Aftab, *A Parent's Guide to the Internet*, 137.

9. Adapted from *Get CyberSavvy! The DMA's Guide to Parenting Skills for the Digital Age: Online Basics, Behavior and Privacy* (Washington, D.C.: The Direct Marketing Association, 1997), 22.

10. Aftab, *A Parent's Guide to the Internet*, 128.

Chapter 6: Creating a Digital Toolbox

1. Patrick Houston, "Survey: Few Parents Use Filtering Software," posted 1 December 1997 at http://www.zdnet.com/zdnn/content/zdnn/1201/249786.html.

2. Remarks by President Bill Clinton at White House Summit for the Internet, Washington, D.C., 16 July 1997.

3. Center for Democracy and Technology, Internet Family Empowerment White Paper, 16 July 1997, at http://www.cdt.org/speech/empower.html.

4. "Virtual Toolbox Ready to Block Internet Porn," *Bellingham Herald*, 17 July 1997, p. C-1.

5. Hitachi, California, Issues Poll on New Media and the Family, CommSciences Inc., Los Angeles, Calif., September 1997, 3–11.

6. Houston, "Survey." For the results of the *Family PC* magazine survey, go to http://www.zdnet.com/familypc/content/kidsafety/results.html.

7. Lorrie Faith Cranor (AT&T Labs-Research) and Paul Resnick (The University of Michigan School of Information), *Internet Online Summit Technology Inventory*, 1997 at http://www.research.att.com/projects/tech4kids.

8. "Why the Internet Is Not Safe for Children," Net Filter Technologies—Kidznet press advisory, 17 January 1997.

9. Aftab, *A Parent's Guide to the Internet*, 171.

10. Center for Democracy and Technology, Internet Family Empowerment White Paper, 16 July 1997, at http://www.cdt.org/speech/empower.html.

11. List adapted from *Internet Online Summit Technology Inventory*, 6.

12. Adapted from "Enough Is Enough Newsletter" 5, no. 2, p. 4.

Chapter 7: Expanding Your Child's Safety Net

1. Mary Lord, "Keeping Your Kids from Internet Demons," *U.S. News & World Report*, 15 December 1997, 38.

2. Clinton, "A Message to Parents."

3. National Center for Education Statistics, 1998, at http://www.nces.ed.gov.

4. Advanced Telecommunications in U.S. Private Schools K–12, *Statistical Analysis Report*, June 1997 (Fast Response Survey System). National Center for Education Statistics (97-394), U.S. Dept. of Education. Available on NCES Web site: http://www.nces.ed.gov.

5. Ibid.

6. National Center for Education Statistics, *Survey of Advanced Telecommunications in U.S. Public Elementary and Secondary Schools, 1995* (February 1996), 3.

7. National Center for Education Statistics, 1998, at http://www.nces.ed.gov.

8. *1997 National Survey of U.S. Public Libraries and the Internet* (Washington, D.C.: American Library Association's Office for Information Technology Policy, 1997).

9. Jeremy Redmon, "Fairfax Schools Consider Barriers to Internet Porn," *Washington Times*, 19 September 1997, p. C5.

10. Lori Gray, "Internet Porn Charge," *Daily News Journal*, 16 December 1997, p. 1.

11. "Man Charged with Viewing Internet Porn at Ohio Library," *Cleveland Plain Dealer*, 28 June 1997.

12. Kathryn Wexler, "Libraries Being Used for X-rated Browsing," *St. Petersburg Times*, 12 March 1977, p. 1A.

13. "School and Library Internet Terminals Used to Access Sexually Explicit Material Every 15 Seconds," N2H2 Filtering Report Press Release, Seattle, 1997, 1.

14. "Surfing Schools: Issues and Answers Regarding Students on the Internet," a White Paper prepared by WatchGuard Technologies, Inc., 6.

15. Zachary Britton, *SafetyNet: Guiding and Guarding Your Children on the Internet* (Eugene, Oreg.: Harvest House, 1998), 60.

16. Cranor and Resnick, *Technology Inventory*.

17. From *Internet Safety Kit* (Fairfax, Va.: Enough Is Enough, 1998).

18. "Child Safety Online," a White Paper prepared by a subcommittee of the Child Advocacy Working Group, Internet Online Summit: Focus on Children, December 1–3, 1997.

19. David Burt, "The ACLU's Intimidation of Librarians," Filtering Facts at www.filteringfacts.org.

20. "Fahrenheit 451.2: Is Cyberspace Burning? How Rating and Blocking Proposals May Torch Free Speech on the Internet," an American Civil Liberties Union Report (ACLU Publications, August 1997), 12.

21. *Mainstream Loudoun v Board of Trustees of the Loudoun County Library*, CA-97-2049-A. The entire document is located at http://www.venable.com/oracle/dismiss.htm.

22. Elizabeth Whitaker, written testimony to the Senate Committee on Commerce, Science, and Transportation (Washington, D.C., 10 February 1998), 2.

23. Adapted from Lazarus and Lipper, *The Parents' Guide to the Information Superhighway*, 21; see also *Parent's Guide to the Internet*.

24. Adapted from *Library Action Manual*, 1,

Chapter 8: It Takes All of Us

1. *Suggested Code of Ethical Conduct for ISPs and OSPs* (Washington D.C.: Enough Is Enough, 1997).

2. William Presecky, "Officials Target Kids' Safety on Internet," *Chicago Tribune*, 17 October 1997, sec. 2, p. 11.

3. "Adult Entertainment Businesses in Indianapolis: An Analysis" (Indianapolis: Dept. of Metropolitan Development, Division of Planning, February 1984), iii.

Appendix D: Pornography on the Internet

1. *Take Action Manual*, 13.
2. Michael Kelly, "We Don't Need New Regulations to Challenge Porn on the Web," *Detroit Free Press* (3 December 1997), p. 13A.

3. UConn Center for Survey Research & Analysis.
4. Lederer, *National Legislation on and International Trafficking in Child Pornography*, 2.

Glossary

Computer and Internet Terms

adult password—A system for adult verification with the purpose of segregating unsuitable Internet content from children. To receive an adult password, one must go through an adult verification process.

blocking/filtering software—Software, such as parental control software, used to block access to inappropriate Internet sites.

bookmark—A saved link to a Web site that has been added to a list of saved links or favorite sites so that you can click on it rather than having to retype the address when revisiting the site.

boot—To start a computer or ready it for use; to load a program into a computer from a disk.

browser—A program that lets you find, see, and hear material on Web pages. Popular browsers include Netscape Navigator, Mosaic, and Microsoft Internet Explorer.

bulletin board service (BBS)—An online computer system that allows the exchange of mail, messages, and file downloading.

CD-ROM Compact Disc-Read Only Memory. A high-capacity optical storage medium.

chat room—A location online that allows users to communicate with each other in real time as opposed to delayed time as with e-mail.

closed systems—A limited network of sites that are rated and categorized by maturity level and quality. Within a closed system, children cannot go beyond the network *white list* of approved Web sites.

cookie—A piece of information about your visit to their site that some Web sites record automatically on your computer. By using a cookie, a Web site operator can determine where you've been and a lot of information about you and your computer. Cookies are not always bad. For example, a cookie remembers that you prefer aisle seats in the front of the airplane.

cruising the Information Superhighway—Surfing the Internet or browsing the Web as you would browse through a library or a catalog.

cyberspace—The electronic areas and communities existing on the Internet and other computer networks, as well as the culture that is developing around them.

domain name—The part of an Internet address to the right of the final dot used to identify the type of organization using the server, such as .gov or .com.

download—To copy a file from one computer system on the Internet to another.

e-mail—A way of sending messages electronically from one computer to another; requires a modem and telephone line connected to your computer.

emoticons—Typewritten characters that allow the user to express emotions or actions, such as this sideways smiley face :-)

engine—See *search engine.*

FAQs (frequently asked questions)—Newsgroups and some Web sites provide newcomers with answers to common questions.

flame—A hostile, strongly worded message that may contain obscene language.

freenet—A community network that provides free online access, usually to local residents, and often includes its own forums and news.

FTP (File Transfer Protocol)—A protocol that enables computers to connect and transfer files back and forth.

GIF (Graphics Interchange Format)—A standard graphic image format found on the Internet.

gigabyte (GB)—A measurement of memory; one GB equals a thousand megabytes (MBs).

gopher—A menu-based tool used for navigation on the Internet.

green space—Approved Web site.

hacker—A person who tries to break into computer systems.

hardware—A term for the actual computer equipment and related machines.

home page—The site that is the starting point on the Web for a particular group or organization.

hot link—A word or graphic that can be clicked with a mouse to bring the user to a new Web site.

HTML (HyperText Markup Language)—A programming language, used for formatting Web pages, that is decoded by a browser and displayed on a computer screen as text or graphics.

hypertext link—Text that can be linked to other text on the Internet by clicking on highlighted words or icons on the screen. The link will take you to related documents or sites.

HyperText Transfer Protocol (HTTP)—A standard used by Web servers to provide rules for moving text, images, sound, video, and other multimedia files across the Internet.

icon—A small picture on a Web page that represents the topic or information category of another Web page.

Information Superhighway—A term first popularized by Vice President Al Gore. A global high-speed network of computers that will serve thousands of users simultaneously. The Superhighway links homes, offices, schools, libraries, medical centers, and so on, so that information can be instantly accessed and transmitted from one computer screen to another.

instant message (IM)—A typed message that takes place in real time, much like a phone conversation.

Internet (Net)—A giant collection of computer networks that connects people and information all over the world. The format of Internet e-mail addresses such as parent@earthlink.com, is easily recognizable.

Internet Relay Chat (IRC)—A multiuse live chat facility. IRC is an area of the Internet comprised of thousands of chat rooms. IRC is run by IRC servers and requires client software to use.

Internet Service Provider (ISP)—A generic term for any company that can connect you directly to the Internet. Ask a friend with Web access to download and print for you a list of ISPs for your area using this Web site: http://www.thelist.com.

JPEG (Joint Partner Experts Group or *Joint Photographic Experts Group)*—A popular file format for graphic images on the Internet.

kilobyte (KB)—A common unit of measurement for memory. One thousand KBs equals one megabyte.

LAN (Local Area Network)—A network of computers, typically limited in size to a single building or floor of a building.

listserv—An e-mail mailing list you subscribe to. It's essentially a discussion group where all messages and responses are e-mailed instead of being posted on a bulletin board.

log off—The act of disconnecting from the Internet.

mailing list—A topical discussion held through e-mail, taking an e-mailed posting from one of its subscribers and forwarding it to other subscribers.

megabyte (MB)—A common measure of computer memory.

megahertz (MHz)—A measurement of speed.

modem—A device installed in your computer or an external piece of hardware that connects your computer to the Internet through a phone line and allows communication between computers.

morph—A computer-generated or enhanced photo.

mouse—A small hand-controlled device for pointing and clicking to make selections on the screen.

Net—See *Internet*.

netiquette—Rules or manners for interacting courteously with others online (such as not typing a message in all capital letters, which is equivalent to shouting).

newsgroups—See *USENET newsgroups*.

Online Service Provider (OSP)—A company such as America Online, MSN, CompuServe, or Prodigy that provides its members access to the Internet, through its own special user interface. Additional services might include chat rooms, children's areas, travel planning, and financial management.

open system—A network of Web sites that are accessible to all users. The user is able to click on hot links to go from one site to the next. Within an open system, children can go beyond the network *white list* of approved Web sites.

password—A secret word or number that must be used to gain access to an online service or to modify software, such as a parental control. See *adult password*.

parental controls—Special features or software that allow parents to control the online activities of children.

Platform for Internet Content Selection(PICS)—An infrastructure for associating labels with Internet content. PICS is a platform on which other rating services and filtering software have been built.

post—To send a message to a newsgroup.

posting—The message sent to a newsgroup.

RAM (random access memory)—The amount of active memory on a computer.

rating service—A service that rates Web sites for content.

real time—"Live" time; the actual time during which something takes place.

search engine—A program that allows you to search through Web sites.

server—A computer that hosts Web sites, chat areas, and newsgroups.

smart card—a standard plastic card that has the ability to store information.

software—A program, or set of instructions, that runs on a computer.

spam—An inappropriate newsgroup posting or junk e-mail.

surfing the Net—Browsing through Web sites as you would browse through a library or a catalog, looking for topics or things that interest you; first coined by Net-mom Jean Armour Polly.

telnet—A means of connecting by way of the Internet to a nonlocal computer.

third-party server—A remote facility, not on your computer. Some companies offer software, located on their server, to which you may subscribe.

uniform resource locator (URL)—The address of a site on the Internet. For example, the URL for the White House is: http://www.whitehouse.gov. Each URL is unique and there are millions of them.

uploading—To send information from *your* computer to another computer.

URL—See *uniform resource locator*.

USENET newsgroups—A system of thousands of special interest groups to which readers can post messages. These messages are then distributed to other computers on the network. Newsgroups are generally offered as a service through Internet Service Providers. USENET is a worldwide collection of newsgroups.

virus—A piece of programming code inserted into other programming that can cause lost or damaged files. Viruses are transmitted by downloading programming from other sites or by using infected floppy disks. The virus may lie dormant until circumstances cause its code to be executed by the computer. Viruses are not passed in text files, only through applications.

white list—A list of green spaces or approved Web sites.

Windows—Microsoft's operating system for IBM–compatible personal computers.

World Wide Web (WWW or Web)—A hypertext-based navigation system on the Internet that lets you browse through a variety of linked resources, using typed commands or clicking on hot links.

Index

In her position at the nonprofit organization Enough Is Enough, **Donna Rice Hughes** played a pioneering role in the national effort to make the Internet safe for children. Enough Is Enough has emerged as the leading organization in the country dedicated to this cause. A Phi Beta Kappa graduate of the University of South Carolina, Donna has spoken extensively and given more than twelve hundred regional, national, and international interviews on the subject of child safety on the Internet. She has also written numerous articles featured in such publications as the *Los Angeles Times,* the *Washington Times,* and *USA Today.*

Donna was instrumental in the development and promotion of a three-pronged strategy for Internet safety that involves the public, the technology industry, and law enforcement sharing the responsibility to protect children on the Internet. This approach has been adopted by many industry and government leaders.

In 1997 Donna represented Enough Is Enough on the steering committee for the Internet Online Summit: Focus on Children and is currently on the executive committee of the Summit's public education campaign, "America Links Up."

Donna and her husband, Jack, live in northern Virginia. Through her marriage to Jack, Donna has two stepchildren, Sean and Mindy.

Pamela T. Campbell is a freelance writer and editor with more than eighteen years of diverse experience in the publishing industry. Currently, in her position as director of publications for the American Association of Christian Counselors, she oversees *Christian Counseling Today* magazine and *Marriage and Family: A Christian Journal.*

Pam is the author of numerous books, including *Simple Blessings,* and she lives in a suburb of Chicago with her husband, Stan, and her Sheltie, Thera.

Visit the Kids Online Web site at http://www.protect kids.com